The
WICKED
GOOD
Book

A Guide to
MAINE LIVING

The
WICKED
GOOD
Book

STEPHEN GLEASNER

Illustrated by Patrick Corrigan

Down East
MAINE

To my daring research assistants
Clark and Meg and to Illya who
makes art possible.

ISBN 978-1-60893-181-1
Library of Congress
Cataloging-in-Publication
Data available upon request.
Design by Lynda Chilton

Printed in the United States
5 4 3 2 1

BOOKS·MAGAZINE·ONLINE
www.downeast.com

Distributed to the trade by National Book Network

Contents

Introduction --- 7

1   Moose Defense 101 -- 9

2   Cooped Up Like a Chicken ------------------------------- 11

3   A Walk on the Wild Side --------------------------------- 15

4   Bloom and Bark Kingdom ------------------------------- 20

5   The Maine Night Sky ------------------------------------- 25

6   Digging for Clams --- 28

7   The Mysterious and Elusive Fiddlehead ----------------- 30

8   Hypnotized By Lobster ---------------------------------- 32

9   What's Wild and Blue? ---------------------------------- 35

10   Panning for Gold --------------------------------------- 38

11   The Ice Cometh --- 41

12   To Climb or Not to Climb Maine's Highest Mountain? --------------- 45

13   Stalking Night Crawlers --------------------------------- 50

14   Gone Fishing --- 53

15   Bike the Down East Sunrise Trail ------------------------------ 58

16   Splitting Firewood Like a Lumberjack -------------------------- 61

17   11 Books Every Mainer Should Read --------------------------- 63

18   How to Build a Rustic Shelter ---------------------------------- 67

19   How to Survive a Fall Through Ice ------------------------------ 69

20   Making Fire: Getting in Touch with Your Inner Caveman --------------- 73

21   Go-Cart Racing -- 78

22   The Roll Back--- 78

23   How to Build a Survival Shelter -------------------------------- 83

24   A Canoe and the Man Who Built One --------------------------- 86

25   Making a Long Bow Like Robin Hood --------------------------- 91

26   X Marks the Spot -- 94

27   Build a Stone Arch --- 97

28   Skipping Stones --- 99

29   Toss Some Apples --- 101

30   Rat Hunting --- 103

31   The Moxie Rocket --- 105

32   Maine Roller Derby -- 108

33   Pond Hockey -- 111

34   How to Keep a Knife Sharpe ---------------------------------- 115

35   The Woodcock --- 119

Introduction

MY LITERARY AGENT, AND GENERALLY COOL GUY, TRIS COBURN, CALLED ME OUT OF THE BLUE ONE WINTER DAY TO TELL ME ABOUT THIS GREAT IDEA FOR A NOSTALGIC, PRACTICAL, AND IRREVERENT GUIDE TO GETTING THE MOST OUT OF LIVING IN THE PINE TREE STATE. I wasn't sure what to make of the project in the beginning, but the more I thought about it, the more I liked the idea.

This is a book for those who never want to grow up. It's for the kid in all of us. And it's also for those of us who love Maine from dawn to dusk. Maybe you've never climbed Katahdin. Well maybe this is the year to climb the highest mountain in Maine. Maybe you've always wanted to make a fire with a magnifying glass or a stick spun in a pine board with a sapling and a shoestring. Now's the time. Maybe your palms itch to pan for gold. Maybe you've always wanted to make your own long bow, to hold a piece of history in your hands and to feel the same power as you draw it back, that people felt before the invention of gunpowder.

And maybe you've always longed to build your own canoe and paddle down a forgotten stretch of the Kennebec.

Without this book I might not have done some of the wonderful things I've done. Looking back on the whole thing, I never spent much money, and I mostly did things because I decided to do them.

My advice to you: Don't wait for a call from an agent to do some of these wicked good Maine things. Adventure awaits you out there in this wonderful state of Maine. ■

1 Moose Defense 101

THERE ARE FOUR KINDS OF MOOSE: A BULL, A COW, A CALF, AND THE DANGER-OUS KIND.

Big moose look funny and they're not carnivorous, so, you might wonder, why are they dangerous?

A bull moose is most irritable in the fall, when he is look-ing for a mate. He often stops eating during the rutting season, which doesn't help his already ornery nature. A bull moose has two things on its minds during this time: fighting and mating. Bulls want to mate with the females and fight with the males. (Sometimes nature is not unlike a saloon.) A male moose that mistakes a person for a rival male might charge — they see you as a threat. It's your job to reassure the charging moose that you want to be somewhere else and aren't looking for a date with his lady moose.

A cow moose is most dangerous in the spring and early summer when she has a calf with her. Don't approach any moose, but approaching a baby will invoke the wrath of its mother.

Canine Clash

Moose have an instinctual hatred for dogs — wolves and coyotes have had a long relationship with moose: they eat them. Because domesticated dogs are direct descendants of the wolf, dogs strike an espe-cially bad chord with the huge herbivores. If you are walking your dog, do your best to discourage it from barking, lunging, or snarling at any moose.

Huge Herbivore

A full-grown bull moose can weigh up to 1,500 pounds (that's more than five NFL linemen in full battle gear). The shoulder of a large moose, which stands six to seven feet, is taller than most people. He can also kick with huge force, and, depending on the time of year, he might have a huge rack of antlers.

Any moose, of course, walking toward you, pinning its ears back, grunting, shaking its head back and forth, and stomping its feet is bad news. And a charging moose is even worse. Although there is some good news here: most charges are bluffs. And you should also never challenge a moose with sticks or stones or shouts. And never try to look like you have a huge rack on your head.

Your safest bet with a moose: snap photos from a safe distance. ■

Large Moose Alert

Here are some practical trips on avoiding dangerous moose encounters.

✔ Back away. Or better yet, run! This should send a clear message. Whatever you do, you should never hold your hands out to the side and sway back and forth like you have a huge rack of antlers on your head. Also, don't paw the ground with your foot. Do your best to look as un-moose-like as you can — which shouldn't be too difficult.

✔ Climb a tree. But don't leave any body parts dangling within antler reach. Another option is to get behind a single tree or a group of trees, preferably closer together than the animal's rack.

✔ If all else fails and the moose makes contact with your body, ball up, cover your head with your arms, and play dead. If you play dead, these will be the longest, loneliest moments of your life — well besides being stuck in traffic on Route 1 on a summer's day. But there is no way around this. Make sure the moose is gone before getting up. You don't want to reintroduce yourself as a threat. Moose often come back to check on your status.

2 Cooped Up Like a Chicken

WHEN I FIRST GOT CHICKENS, THEY STARTED LAYING EGGS IN THEIR STRAW-FILLED NESTING BOXES. Nothing unusual about that. But then something happened to my feelings about eggs.

The first fried egg from our new chickens made me slightly uncomfortable. In fact it grossed me out a bit. But I ended up forcing the egg down. It was, after all, a perfectly good egg.

But here's the straight scoop on why I suddenly became egg shy: Where do eggs come from? They come from the same orifice that spits out chicken poop.

Obviously, this information took a little getting used to. My egg use dropped off.

But the wonderful thing about owning chickens is that you quickly put aside childish, squeamish thoughts when you think about fresh eggs from you own backyard.

So, let's start with the chicken: Hen's don't cost much. Twelve to fifteen dollars will get you a laying hen in her prime. If you are the patient type, you can buy a baby chick for less than three dollars, but don't expect omelets any time soon. It takes a

Lord of the Roost

We have a rooster named Chip. He's about as big as a pigeon. But Chip performs all his rooster duties as if he were an ostrich. Most of his day is spent looking regal and important. He begins the day with a multitude of announcements, signaling loudly that, yes, the sun has risen again. He spends the rest of the day just looking important all over the place: this includes the ridge of my workshop — until a hawk attacked him there. He nearly died from the attack and spent a week in a cat-carrier in our bathroom convalescing. Since his near-death

Lord of the Roost

(continued)

experience, Chip's displays of importance are now limited to less exposed areas. Oh, and, yes, he's a hen's man, which is probably the most important function of his day.

chicken four to six months until she starts producing eggs. You should have an egg in the next day or two once she sets up shop. You can then expect an average bird in her prime to lay just under one egg a day. Most days they lay one. About once a week they skip a day (it almost sounds biblical, but even chickens need a Sabbath day about once a week), and every now and then, they lay two eggs in one day. Their egg production drops about 30 percent in the second laying season and it continues to slide each year after. Expect a couple good laying years out of a hen before she stops laying all together.

So, what do you do with a hen that has stopped producing eggs? In the past, we've had good luck with putting our old hens in *Uncle Henry's* under "Free for the Taking," and they become soup for somebody who wants to put in the time to pluck and prepare a bird that's skimpy on meat. Sometimes, though, I butcher one myself. One time I killed and plucked an old rooster that had gotten into the habit of attacking people. Mean roosters are only good for the soup pot.

When chickens get older, they slow down on egg production. All of them slow down in the winter unless you "force them" with artificial lighting to extend their day, but this stresses the birds. We just try to cut back our egg consumption in the winter, but, sooner of later, I end up at the supermarket, having to decide, ironically, which kind of chicken I want my eggs to come from: a free-range chicken, a free-range organic chicken, or a cage-free natural chicken. Every time this happens, I think, I just want the eggs from the chickens out in the barn! I like them. I like the noises they make. I like their beady little eyes. And no matter which eggs I buy at the supermarket, the yolks always look pale in comparison to our own.

One of the biggest challenges with owning chickens is they need a coop to roost out of the elements. And you need to

Idioms That Come from Chickens

Bad egg: less than honest person

Brood over it: to worry over a problem

Chicken feed: a small amount of something, especially money

Chicken scratch: poor handwriting

Chickens have come home to roost: the past is catching up with you

Cock and bull story: tall tales and elaborate lies

Cock sure: to brag

Do chickens have lips?: dumb question that gets a dumb answer

Don't be a chicken: taunting someone who is being cowardly

Don't count your chickens before they hatch: never assume you'll get something; wait until you actually have it

Don't put all your eggs in one basket: don't plan on an outcome before it actually happens

Egg on your face: caught in a lie

Empty nest syndrome: depression and loneliness when children leave home

Feather your nest: saving for the future

Flew the coop: gone

Go to bed with the chickens: a person who goes to bed at sundown, the same time as chickens roost

Hard-boiled: tough attitude

Hen house: large number of females living in the same house

Henpecked: to subject a person to persistent nagging and domination

If it ain't chickens, it's feathers: there are always problems in life

Mother hen: very protective

Not a spring chicken anymore: a person who is getting older, and will most probably retire to Maine

Pecking order: a social hierarchy among people in a particular group

Ruffle your feathers: when something annoys you

Rules the roost: a person who makes all the decisions in a group

Run around like a chicken with its head cut off: to be in a frantic state

Scarce as hen's teeth: extremely hard to find

Shake a tail feather: get moving

Something to crow about: exciting news to tell

Sunny side up: cheerful attitude

Tastes like chicken: to describe the taste of any number of other meats

Walking on eggshells: treading softly where certain people are concerned

Famous Literary Chicken Quotes

"A hen is only an egg's way of making another egg."
Samuel Butler

"I want there to be no peasant in my kingdom so poor that he cannot have a chicken in his pot every Sunday."
Henry IV

"Business is never so healthy as when, like a chicken, it must do a certain amount of scratching for what it gets."
Henry Ford

"It is better to be the head of a chicken than the rear end of an ox."
Japanese Proverb

"Ain't nobody here but us chickens."
Louis Jordan

"Boys, I may not know much, but I know chicken poop from chicken salad."
Lyndon B. Johnson

"A chicken in every pot."
The 1928 Republican Party campaign slogan

"Don't have a pot to put it in."
The 1928 Democratic Party response slogan

keep their water from freezing. You can buy an electric heater that sits below the automatic waterer to keep the water from freezing. Most chickens, like most Mainers, can put up with the winter just fine if they have a place to get away from the wind, rain, and snow. You also want to make sure that the coop is safe from predators. Everything eats chickens: ospreys, owls, hawks, eagles, raccoons, weasels, and even dogs. The life of a chicken is a tough one. Rats are also a problem. Sooner or later, if you have chickens, you will probably have rats. Chickens don't have the greatest table manners. But having rats isn't such a bad thing, I have turned my rat problem into a bit of a hobby (see Chapter 30 on Rat Hunting).

Like most people who own backyard chickens, we usually reach a point when we have more eggs than we know what to do with. When this happens, we put a little sign out in front of the house and neighbors stop by in droves to pick up a dozen or two. But we still have way too many eggs.

Which makes me think about that conundrum about which came first, the chicken or the egg. At such times, I'm almost sure the egg really did come first. ■

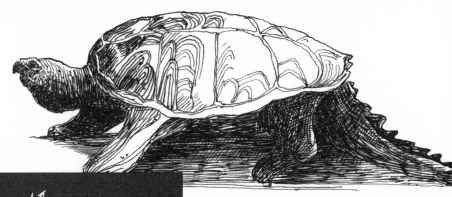

3 A Walk on the Wild Side

THERE ARE SO MANY OPPORTUNITIES IN MAINE TO EITHER SPOT OR RUN ACROSS WILDLIFE. HERE'S A LIST OF SOME OF THE INDIGENOUS FAUNA YOU ARE MOST LIKELY TO FIND. Some, like the skunk, may be a nuisance; others, like the snake, may cause a panic attack, but what they all have in common is that they're Mainers, just like the other denizens of the state.

Snapping Turtles *(Chelydra serpentine)*

Snappers are prehistoric looking and are sometimes irascible towards humans, but I guess you can be when you've been around for 90 million years. They have highly mobile heads and powerful beak-like jaws capable of crushing a broomstick. And snappers like to cross roads for some reason. Sometimes they even cross Interstate 95. Mostly it's because the female is looking for a safe place to lay her eggs. Female snappers can mate and keep the male's sperm viable for up to two years. Baby snappers are born between nine to eighteen weeks after the female decides to fertilize her eggs, and depending on the weather. Snappers prefer their own company and are not very social. They can live as long as forty years, happily avoiding each other's company as much as possible.

Snakes

You can rest easy about snakes in Maine. Maine has no venomous snakes. It is home to the eastern milk snake, the northern water snake, the eastern garter snake, the maritime garter snake, the eastern and northern ribbon snake, the northern brown snake, northern redbelly snake, northern ringneck snake, the smooth green snake (electric lime green!), and the northern black racer. According to NERD (the New England Reptile Distributor) owner Kevin McCurley, the last timber rattler seen in Maine was in 1901. NERD offers a three-hundred-dollar reward for knowledge of any confirmed rattler (or copperhead) reports in New England. Snakes bring out the worst in people; a simple garter snake in dry leaves can sound like a rattler when it vibrates its tail. But snakes help keep the rodent population under control. And it's also good to know that it's nearly impossible to come across any venomous snakes (no snakes are poisonous) in Maine. So don't kill any snakes.

Ticks

This external parasite is on the rise in Maine. But here's something you may not know about these pests: ticks are not insects but arachnids, a class of arthropods that also includes mites, spiders, and scorpions. And ticks are divided into two groups: hard bodied and soft bodied, both of which are capable of transmitting pathogenic agents. Ticks are parasites that feed by latching onto an animal host, imbedding their mouthparts into the host's skin, and sucking the blood (not unlike another Maine denizen named Barnabas Collins). Ticks are responsible for at least ten different known diseases, including Lyme disease, Rocky Mountain spotted fever, babesiosis, and more recently, anaplasmosis and ehrlichiosis. The biggest danger ticks pose, specifically the deer tick (*Ixodes scapularis*), is that they carry Lyme disease. If a tick attaches to you, use tweezers to remove it. Grab the tic as close to their head as possible. Use even pressure to pull it off. Do not use a match or poison. Disinfect the site after the tick is removed. If the tick is irritated, it might regurgitate, increasing the danger of a Lyme infection. Deer ticks range in size from something as large as the period at the end of this sentence to almost an eighth of an inch in length. According to the Centers for Disease Control, the incidence of Lyme disease has more than tripled since 1995. If you get a strange rash or feel like you have the flu after a tick bite, see you doctor immediately. If you get treatment quickly, you can eliminate the infection.

Fisher (*Martes pennanti*)

A member of the weasel family, fisher males weigh between eight and thirteen pounds, the females between four and six. They are omnivorous and will eat almost anything, usually rodents, rabbits, hares, and birds, though rarely fish. They also eat carrion and are among the few predators that can kill porcupines. Fishers are fierce fighters and can hold their own against much larger animals. A male's territory can be up to thirty square miles, a female's up to ten. Fishers can be active day or night. They tend to be solitary and defend their territories. They were once hunted for their lustrous, chocolate-brown fur, so their numbers have been reduced greatly in the United States.

Porcupines (*Erethizon dorsatum*)

The name porcupine comes from the French, "*porc espin*," which translates roughly to "quill pig." Porcupines make an oinking

sound when they waddle around. They are mostly nocturnal, but are sometimes seen walking around in the daytime. Porcupines like salt and will sometimes chew on canoe paddle handles while you are asleep. They can weigh as much as thirty-five pounds and are good climbers. They are born with soft quills that harden a few days after birth. This explains how they are born, but how they get close enough to mate is another story.

Skunks *(Mephitis mephitis)*

These polecats are part of the weasel family and are opportunistic eaters with a varied diet. Skunks are nocturnal and often use burrows of other animals or holes under tree stumps or buildings. Sometimes they use their long front claws to build their own dens. Skunks are legendary for their horrible smelling predator deterrent spray. The spray is an oily liquid produced by glands under its large tail. To employ this scent bomb, a skunk turns around and blasts its foe with the foul mist, which can travel as far as ten feet. Females often remain inactive throughout the winter, but males usually emerge from their dens to feed during mild intervals. A winter den usually consist of six females and their young. They like communal living. A male may sometimes overwinter in a den with females, but he usually lives alone. Dogs are also fascinated with these polecats. If you or your dog gets sprayed, washing with tomato juice is a way to deal with the smell, but don't expect the smell to leave right away.

Bats

Maine is home to the big brown bat, little brown bat, northern long-eared bat, tri-colored bat, and eastern small-footed bat. In 2011 Maine became the last New England state to report a bat disease called white-nose-syndrome (WNS). WNS devastates colonies of hibernating bats. Without a healthy bat population, flying insect numbers increase — that means more mosquitoes and blackflies! Bats are nocturnal and eat bugs on the fly using sophisticated sonar to locate and catch insects in midair. Bats are generally not a nuisance, but if they start nesting in your house, they can cause problems. They live in colonies, so if you see a bat go into your house, you might want to call a professional. If you seal the openings during the day, the bats will be trapped in your house, a situation you don't want. If done at the proper time of year, the bats will have a good chance of finding a new dwelling.

Wild Turkeys

When you live in Maine, a gaggle of wild turkeys strutting through the backyard is a common sight. Although this wasn't always true. There were no wild turkeys in Maine until 1977 and 1978, when the Maine Department of Inland Fisheries and Wildlife obtained forty-one gobblers from Vermont and released them into the southern towns of York and Eliot. Now, the wild gobbler is North America's largest upland game bird. Average adult hens (the females) weigh between eight and twelve pounds and adult toms (the males) between ten and twenty — but some toms can weigh as much as twenty-five pounds. The bristle-like feathers that protrude from the male's chest can grow to a length of more than twelve inches. Beards are present on about 10 percent of the hens, however, they are thinner and shorter than those of adult males. Male gobblers' heads are generally bare and blue with a hint of pink and red, but during the mating season, the gobbler's crown swells and turns white and its wattles become large and bright red. The hens' heads are somewhat feathered with smaller, darker feathers extending up from the back of the neck. Wild turkey plumage is more iridescent than domestic turkeys, and their tail feathers are tipped with brown rather than white. Turkeys can fly up to sixty miles per hour and a distance of one mile. ■

4 Bloom and Bark Kingdom

WHEN PEOPLE THINK OF MAINE, THE
FIRST PLANT THAT COMES TO MIND IS
THE LUPINE — SEEING THEIR COLORFUL
ROADSIDE SWATHES BLOOMING IN JUNE
IS A HEAVENLY SIGHT. But here is a list of other flora
in the Pine Tree State that are just as abundant and interesting,
but maybe not as lavish as the lupine.

Seaweed

You might not think of seaweed as part of Maine's flora, but
there's a fellow in Steuben who has been making his living harvesting seaweed for the past forty years. He takes to the ocean
with a knife, a small rowboat, and a wetsuit. He gardens as the
ocean tosses his boat about and the surf tries to knock him down.
His name is Larch Hanson, but he's become known as the "Seaweed Man." He harvests, dries, and sells one of the oldest family
of plants on earth: kelp, which is great roasted and served with
popcorn. He also harvests badderlocks, which is good in soup,
dulse, which when roasted makes a crunchy snack chip, bladder-

wrack, and digitata, which is similar to kombu, and something called *Ascophyllum nodosum* for garden fertilizer. Thirty pounds of seaweed dries down to about three pounds, which, Larch says, lasts the typical seaweed-eating family about six months.

Eastern White Pine

There are 115 species of pines. The eastern white pine is the state tree of both Maine and Michigan. Eastern white pine needles are between three and five inches long and grow in bundles of five. The cones are between four and seven inches long and the tree grows about one foot per year. The lumber is soft, light, and easily cut with sharp tools. The wood has been highly valued since the early sailing days. In 1691, King George I of England enacted the Broad Arrow Policy, which stated that all large white pines within three miles of the water were marked as property of the Royal Navy and were to used as masts for its sailing ships. Today the tree is still a valuable lumber, and white pine that is not good enough for lumber is turned into pulp for paper products and ceiling tiles. Birch bark canoe builders still use pinesap to waterproof seams. The needles have five times the amount of vitamin C as the same weight of lemons. The best way to get the vitamin C is by steeping young needles in hot water to make a tea. The inner bark is edible — the closer to the wood the more palatable it will be. Fry it in a pan with oil until crispy, like a potato chip. Note: gathering pine bark is a sticky process. The tree must be fresh and healthy. It only takes a couple days after the tree is felled for the bark to lose its culinary appeal.

Maple and Birch

Everyone knows that maple syrup comes from maple trees and some are lucky enough to get the real thing. But you might not know that it takes forty to forty-five gallons of sap to make a single gallon of syrup. And also that birch also makes a sweet sap and that both maple and birch sap can be enjoyed right out of the bucket without even boiling it. Don't expect it to be as sweet as the boiled syrup, but it tastes great straight from the tree, is rich in vitamins and minerals, and is supposed to boost the immune system. Sap season is very short. Often snow still covers the ground. When the days start to warm and the nights are still snappy, look for the beginning of buds on the trees. When the buds start, the sap is running. Or you can just look as you drive down the road. When you start to see buckets hanging from trees, it's sugar time!

Poison Ivy

Poison ivy is a vine that creeps along the ground and climbs trees. It's famous for having three shiny leaves that secrete an irritant oil, called urushiol, that can cause reactions serious enough for a hospital visit. If you have raised red skin, which has little clear-bubbled blisters, it's most likely poison ivy. And the oil is very potent. If you got the oil on a rake handle in the fall and don't wash it off, you can get reinfected the next spring when you pick up the same rake. Dermatologists estimate about 15 percent of people are immune to poison ivy, but most are sensitive to it, some severely. If you know that you have gotten into the plant, rinse the affected area with alcohol, then wash very well with lots of soap. If you get it washed early, you might be able to avoid a reaction. My great-grandfather was very allergic. Someone told him if he ate the three leaves, he would never be bothered by it again. He nearly died. Don't eat poison ivy!

Jewelweed *(Also Called Touch-Me-Not)*

Lots of people don't like jewelweed because it's so good at making more jewelweed — gardeners call this an invasive plant, the rest of us call it a pest. But it's fun to watch bumblebees squeeze into the small orange flowers, which droop under the bumblebee's weight. The plant grows tall and fast from May to October and it spreads its seeds by an ingenious method. The plant has little green seedpods that look like a pregnant guppy, and if you touch a ripe seed with your finger, it explodes like a spring, shooting seeds everywhere. Interestingly enough, the leaves and juice from the stem of jewelweed are used by herbalists to treat poison ivy.

Skunk Cabbage

They really do stink like skunk, hence the name. The pungent-smelling cabbage is found in swamps and wet woods and is one of the first plants to come up in spring. One of the interesting things about skunk cabbage is that it can generate its own heat using an oxygen burning process very similar to that used by animals. The heat in these flowers can reach seventy degrees in the dead of winter, melting the snow around it and attracting beetles and other pollinators. Skunk cabbage tends to favor similar growing conditions as fiddleheads, so look for skunk cabbage and you will often find fiddleheads nearby.

Carnivorous Plants

Maine has its own Little Shop of Horrors when it comes to carnivorous plants. These plants tend to live in nutrient-poor soils so have to do something for food: the smart ones learned to attract bugs and then eat them. Maine has several carnivorous plants. Although not as dramatic as the fast-snapping Venus flytrap, Maine's carnivorous plants get the job done in their own way. They are typically found in wet, boggy areas. The common butterwort (endangered in Maine) stands about six inches tall and has a small purple flower. The sticky hairs on its leaves are what

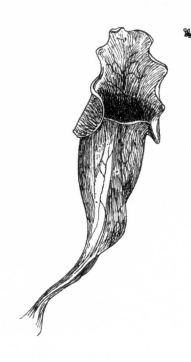

trap insects. Another carnivorous plant is the purple pitcher, which can grow to a foot tall, and can be green, red, or purple. Its leaves curl up as it grows forming a pool that fills with a digestive enzyme. The hairs on the leaf make crawling in easy, but crawling out difficult. The unfortunate insect eventually exhausts itself and falls into the pool of gut-juice and becomes a plant snack. The sundew is our most active meat-eating plant. We have several varieties in Maine, both of which employ movement in their bug capturing. The leaves are covered with sticky hairs that trap the insect, then slowly roll up like a sleeping bag, and digest the bug. It's not the kind of camping trip you come back from.

Puffballs

You have to be careful with mushrooms. There are some that will kill you, but not all wild mushrooms are deadly. The puffball is one that is easy to identify, plentiful, and has a great taste. Mushrooms in general need lots of water, so look for puffballs after rain. You may have seen puffballs that are past their prime: they are roundish and very light, with a leathery skin. If you squeeze them, a puff of what looks like smoke comes out. These are spores and are so small they behave like smoke. The best time to find these fungi is when the inside is creamy and white. Then slice them and fry them in butter. You will forever be on the lookout for edible puffballs for the rest of your days. They are that good. Don't ever eat any mushroom without properly identifying it. Use a good mushroom book, like the *National Audubon Society Field Guide to North American Mushrooms.* ■

5 The Maine Night Sky

LIVING IN MAINE, YOU CAN'T HELP LOOKING UP TO THE STARS. SATELLITE PICTURES SHOW THAT MAINE HAS THE LEAST AMOUNT OF LIGHT POLLUTION OF ANY STATE EAST OF THE MISSISSIPPI. This means we have the darkest skies and the best star viewing of any of the eastern states.

It takes your eyes between ten and thirty minutes to fully adjust so you can get the most out of your star viewing. The average person in Maine can see between 1,500 and 2,000 stars with the naked eye (although they seem countless). Humans have found patterns (constellations) to help clarify the different groups of stars. So it can be fun to lie on your back at night and feel the overwhelming mystery of the stars overhead. The night sky patterns don't change, at least not in any real sense, in a human lifetime. Change is only appreciable over thousands of years.

It's so easy to get to know the sky a little better and you don't need anything but your mind. You don't even need a tele-

Northern Lights

The northern lights depend solely upon solar flare activity. As solar activity increases (it works on an eleven-year cycle), the radiation flowing around the Earth's atmosphere creates a glow (colors vary) in the northern night sky. If you hear about solar activity in the news, look north into the night sky for the northern lights.

Heavenly Signs

There are eighty-eight constellations in the sky. From Maine, at one time or another, we can see roughly two thirds of them. One of the most important constellations is the Big Dipper, which is strange because it is not a constellation at all, but something called an asterism (a prominent pattern or group of stars). The Big Dipper is part of a constellation called the Big Bear. The Big Dipper's outer ladle stars point to Polaris, the North Star, which actually isn't the brightest star; it's just famous because it's directly above the North Pole and can help find directions. If you are facing the North Star, you are looking north. East is to your right, south is behind you, and west is to your left. So without a compass you know where the sun will come up (east) and set (west). The North Star forms the end of the handle of the Little Dipper.

scope or binoculars. They are for seeing individual objects far away. The constellations are all visible to the naked eye.

The night sky might look like a jumble of twinkling dots scattered randomly about in the dark, but constellations help make the patterns more meaningful. Stars that make up the constellations are actually suns from other solar systems (although many stars are binaries with another star orbiting them or they can even be two stars orbiting each other) that can be over a thousand light years away from the Earth.

Moonrise and Sunrise

You might not believe this, but the moon on the horizon is the same size as the moon overhead, same with the sun or any other celestial body in the sky. They look much bigger just as they rise, but this is an optical illusion. How the illusion works is a subject of much debate, but trees or buildings on the horizon are not to blame (some say the illusion is caused by something called the Ponzo Illusion, a trick of perspective). The same illusion happens at sea, where there are no trees or buildings. Also, the atmosphere does not magnify the bodies rising in the sky, as one theory suggests. Try taking a picture of the moon as it rises, and one later when it's overhead. The moon will take up the same amount of the image if you use the same magnification. If you hold a caliper (or any kind of measuring device) at arm's length and measure the moon on the horizon and then when it is overhead, it will measure the same.

The back part of the Big Dipper points to a star called Deneb, which is part of the Swan, as well as one of the stars that makes up the asterism called the Summer Triangle.

Deneb is about 1,500 light years away from the Earth.

To get an idea how far this is, let's look at the speed of light. Light travels at 186,282 miles per second (although, truthfully, the speed of light is never constant unless in a vacuum). The Earth is about 25,000 miles around at the equator. So, if you traveled at the speed of light for one second, you would go around the world more than seven times. That's pretty fast, but even at this speed, light takes about eight minutes to get from our sun to the Earth. The light from Deneb left there more than one thousand years before Columbus sailed across the Atlantic. The light you see from Deneb today is from ancient history. Deneb looks small, but it's actually fifty thousand times brighter than our sun.

In the summer look for these constellations:

Aquila the Eagle
Cygnus the Swan
Scorpius the Scorpion
Delphinus the Dolphin
The Summer Triangle (asterism):
the three stars Deneb, Vega, and Altair

In the winter look for:

Orion the Hunter
Taurus the Bull
Gemini the Twins
Cassiopeia the Queen
Canis Major the Big Dog
Canis Minor the Little Dog

There are more, but these are the easier to find. A summer constellation might be visible in the winter, but it would require viewing at a less desirable hour, like 4 a.m. (the same holds true for the winter constellations in summer). The constellations, in their season, should be visible in the night sky a couple hours after sunset. ■

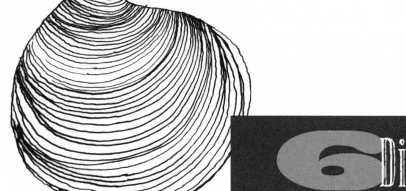

6 Digging for Clams

Know When to Clam Up, and When Not to

Clams under two inches across must be returned to the wild for some more mud time.

Each clam filters between eight and ten gallons of water in a single day, which helps keep our waters clean. We take care of clams and their mud flats when we are not steaming and eating them.

FOOD. Sometimes you think it might all come from Hannaford. We forget in our fast-paced, modern life that someone, somewhere had to grow it, harvest it — or even hunt for it with a rake!

If you've ever seen a bent-over figure on a mud flat, you can be pretty sure he or she is digging for clams. Now, you can get a clam out of the mud with a gloved hand, or you can use a rake. But you'll need to get a license if you want to do any serious clamming. In most cases the local town office can help you with this. Otherwise you can get a day pass or a season pass.

The Digging

Go to a clam flat about an hour before the low tide. Wolfe's Neck Woods State Park, only a couple miles from L.L. Bean and downtown Freeport, is a good spot. When the mudflats are healthy (no red tide warnings), you can clam in the park without a license or any fee, other than admission to the park. (Depending on the tide, you might get a couple of hours of wicked good clamming.)

First thing to do is to look for the clams' breathing holes — the holes look like someone stuck a finger in the mud. The clam's neck looks like a snorkel. It is the most obvious part of the clam outside of its shell, but the neck is just for breathing. The foot is on the other end of the clam. It uses its foot to dig and move in the mud.

Remember: tides come in and out twice a day, so arrive about an hour before low tide. You are allowed to keep one peck of steamers for each person, which is about two gallons.

Wolfe's Neck is a good raking flat since the mud is too dense to just stick your hand down through. And you should wear boots since the flats can be full of broken shells.

Once you find a breathing hole, start digging! You may have to pry slabs of thick dense mud loose, but finding a clam buried in its golden muck is what you're after.

Oh, and you'll have to put up with the pesky gulls.

And this work is back-breaking and messy and incredibly slow. Plus, you'll smell like the low tide and itch from the bugs.

It's hard work and you have to know what you're doing. Clamming is definitely a skill. But it's well worth it — just think of those steamers in butter! ■

Wanted: Dead or Alive!

You can verify if a clam is still alive if the neck moves when touched. If the shell is open, tap on the shell; if the shell closes, that clam is alive. Also check for any clams that have moved out — those shells will be filled with mud. If a clam doesn't open after you steam it, don't eat it! This means it died before it was cooked. Dead clams can make you seriously ill! If you want to get rid of the grit in clams, they need to soak for a while in clean saltwater. But don't do what I did with my five clams, which took me two hours to gather. I kept changing the water, but never let them sit out in the air. They all died before I planned to cook them the next day. I talked to a lady who sells lobsters and steamers. "They drowned," she told me. "Think about it. Clams live in a place that gets aired out twice a day. They need to breath." I drowned my five steamers. It was a fitting finish to my clamming lesson.

7 The Mysterious and Elusive Fiddlehead

THERE'S A LOT OF SECRECY THAT SURROUNDS THE EDIBLE FRONDS OF THE GREEN FIDDLEHEAD. I asked several of my neighbors before the snow melted where I might find a good patch of the edible fern. My phone calls were not returned. Even the old-fashioned way of showing up on a neighbor's doorstep brought no further enlightenment.

"Fiddleheads," I asked, "where can I find a patch?"

My neighbor, who's lived in Maine all his life, just laughed.

All that my neighbor would say on finding a patch of fiddleheads is that their growing season is timed perfectly with the swarming of blackflies. If the flies bite, the fiddleheads are busting through the new spring dirt. He even, in a whisper, let me in on further hidden knowledge: As a young boy, he'd planted a bunch under a big shady tree and that every year after that the patch just got bigger and bigger.

But he wouldn't say where the patch was.

As I was leaving, he offered this: "Look for skunk cabbage; fiddleheads like the same kind of soil."

Hunting for fiddleheads is a kind of Maine spring ritual, when a bunch of hardy New Englanders take to meadows and riverbanks in search of that elusive furled baby fern. It's a fast season, so if you see your first blackfly and you don't know where your fiddlehead patch is hidden, you're probably going to have to buy your ferns at the local grocery store or farmers' market.

Which isn't all that bad. ■

Ostrich Ferns

Lots of ferns look like the head of a fiddle when they are sprouting up out of the ground, but you don't want to eat just any old fern. Make sure the fiddleheads you pick are ostrich ferns. The way to tell is by the deep channel that runs down the inside of the stalks. Other kinds of ferns, although they may have a fiddlehead look, can be toxic — so be careful.

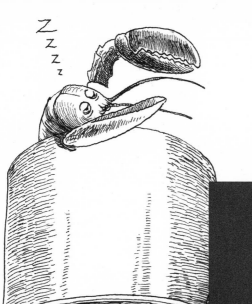

8 Hypnotized By Lobster

MAINE IS THE LAND OF BOILED AND STEAMED LOBSTER. The ubiquitous and iconic crustacean is on our license plates. It is on those silly bibs at lobster shacks. It has a festival devoted to it every August in Rockland. And as a fishing industry, it still pulls a good haul (in 2011, Maine lobster landings topped at 100 million pounds), unlike other fish stocks in the sea.

So I should have know better than to ask a fellow who runs a lobster wholesaling operation whether he had ever hypnotized a lobster. The look of discomfort on his face should have been enough to drop the subject.

But like the ubiquitous "bug," I have a hard shell. So I kept shelling for an answer.

Let's put all the mumbo-jumbo aside for one moment and look at the "science" (if there really is any) behind hypnotizing a lobster before you drop it into a pot — or else amuse your out-of-state friends with lobster tricks.

It turns out that there is a serious debate being waged as to whether lobsters can really be hypnotized. One scientist I spoke

Lobster Lore to Impress

A berried lobster is a female carrying eggs under her tail.

A female lobster is called a hen.

A male lobster is called a cock.

A ghost trap is a lobster trap that has come loose from its buoy but still continues to trap the bugs.

A lobster that had lost both its claws is called a pistol.

A female lobster carrying eggs under her tail is called an egger.

A lobster with only one claw is called a cull.

Lobster liver is called tomalley.

A lobster is a decapod, a ten-legged crustacean.

Lobster Parts

Antenna: Used to search for food as it walks across the seabed.

Great Chelipeds: The claw-bearing front legs. One is called the ripper claw, the other the crusher claw.

Stalked Eye: The eye's surface resembles graph paper and each square is the end of a light-reflecting tube.

Carapace: The body shell of the lobster from the eyes to the tail. To legally kepp a lobster, it must be at least 3 ¼ inches long and no bigger than 5 inches.

Rostrum: This hard shell is used to protect the lobster's eyes.

Uropods: These are the outer pair of tail fins that lobsterman notch if it's an egg-bearing female.

Abdomen: These segments are called somites.

Telson: This is the central tail fin.

Swimmerets: These feathery appendages are also known as pleopods, and help the lobster swim.

Making of a Myth

Live lobsters are not red. Most are either greenish black or orange or yellow or white, some are even a very rare blue. Lobsters turn red only when they are cooked.

to said that a lobster can be "tonically immobilized," but not hypnotized. As far as I can tell, tonic immobilization just means that after being rubbed on the top of its shell, just behind its eyes, the lobster seems to lose any will to move and can be stood on its beak and claws in a kind of tripod arrangement. And the lobster seems content to just stay like this, balanced on its beak and claws. But I don't speak lobster, so it's really hard to say what is on the mind of a tonically immobilized lobster that has been forced to do a headstand.

Some people swear this ritual makes the meat taste better if the lobster is thrown into the boiling water while still under "hypnosis." We carried out a double-blind taste test on our back porch one evening, and I thought all the boiled lobster tasted great.

Hypnotized or not, I guess the taste buds really know best.

Warning: Leave the rubber bands on the claws of any live lobster. I assume no responsibly for people who get pinched by an improperly "tonically immobilized" lobster. ■

9 What's Wild and Blue?

NO, IT'S NOT THE GULF OF MAINE. We're talking those nutrient-rich blueberries. Those wonderful little wild fruits that are chock-full of antioxidants and bursting with a sweet and tangy taste.

There are numerous farms across the state where you can rake low-bush berries. But a word of warning: These bushes are very low to the ground, nothing like their blue cousins the high-bush blueberries, so this will mean a lot of bending over and stooping. Some people (myself included) don't enjoy long periods of crouching and bending, but the haul of massive quantities of blueberries makes it all worthwhile.

Now when you have decided to "pick" your own blueberries, you are going to have to know how to handle a rake (a many metal-pronged tool that looks like a bear's claw — on steroids). A rake will pick a lot of blueberries in a short time, but it will also pick up leaves and twigs and unripe and over-ripe berries. In other words, the rake

Berries to Cure the Winter Blues

One of the best culinary things to do in the winter, when the days are short and cold and snow is everywhere, is to take out a packet of frozen blueberries, picked and sorted in the long days of summer. Then blend the frozen blueberries with some honey and yogurt and you've got a smoothie to sit by the fire with while the snow falls out in the dark and you dream about summer.

does not properly discriminate between berries you like and junk you don't.

Enter the winnower. The winnower is a loud machine powered by a lawnmower engine. You pour the berries into the machine. They fall down a chute while a steady wind, generated by a squirrel-caged fan, blows away the leaves, twigs, and dried berries. In theory, only ripe berries fall into the container.

The Major Players

The major pollinator of Maine's commercial wild blueberries are honeybees, *Apis mellifera*, which are shipped in on trucks from Florida. Maine's wild blueberry farmers are the second largest customers for pollinating bees in the U.S. (almond farmers in California are the only ones who rent more bees than Mainers). But why does Maine bring in Florida bees? Is this

The Buzz: *About 25,000 species of bees are known throughout the world, and 2,000 species are native to the U.S.*

some kind of strange reciprocity for the Mainers who ship out to the Sunshine State when the first snows fly? No, as it turns out. When Maine blueberries need pollinating in the bloom period, native bees are still waking up, still trying to work up their hive numbers. Florida's bees, on the other hand, are already active. So Maine farmers rent these busy Florida bees. The wooden hives are then placed in the blueberry barrens and the bees fly from plant to plant, pollinating one flower after the other.

Why Burn a Blueberry Field?

Besides pollination, blueberry crops are also maintained by burning the field, which is a fast way to prune the blueberry plant. Because most of the plant actually lives below the soil, burning only gets rid of the top third of the plant. Also the burning kills off pests that interfere with blueberry production. Some farmers mow their fields to within an inch of the ground. This does the same thing as burning, but it does little to eliminate pests. Wild blueberries have a two-year life cycle. The first spring, the plant is pruned. That summer, the plant grows. The next spring the plants flower and are ready for pollination. By July and August, the berries are ready for harvest ■

What Do The Antioxidants in Wild Blueberries Do?

The cells in our body are constantly waging a battle against free radicals — unstable oxygen molecules associated with cancer, heart disease, and the effects of aging. Antioxidants, which are natural substances found in fruits and vegetables, come to the rescue by neutralizing free radicals.

Blackfly Conspiracy

I had read somewhere that the blackfly is the largest pollinator of Maine's wild blueberry crop. I liked the idea, but couldn't find anything to back it up. So I called David Yarborough at the University of Maine's Cooperative Extension. Dave Yarborough knows about blueberries. He's got a Phd in Plant and Soil Sciences and wrote his dissertation on "The effect of hexazinone on species distributions and weed competition in low-bush blueberry fields in Maine."

"No," he replied, with a laugh. "Blackflies don't really help much with the blueberry crop. I think that's something that the Maine Blackfly Breeder's Association started."

10 Panning for Gold

GOLD! IT CONJURES UP THE CALIFORNIA GOLD RUSH OF 1848 WHEN JAMES MARSHALL AND PETER L. Wimmer discovered gold in the tailrace at Sutter's new sawmill on the American River. It also conjures up pirates and kings and pyramids and pharaohs. It's so deeply rooted in the human psyche, it's like it's tattooed on our DNA. Throughout history people have made gold more than real; we've made it magical.

Panning for gold is an adventure that allows you to get in touch with a historical event that profoundly changed the American social, political, and cultural landscape. It's a bit like fishing: Just like your next cast could land a fish, the next pan of gravel might hold a gold nugget.

Maine is not as famous for gold as California, or even Alaska, but Maine is a well-respected place to prospect.

Gold can be anywhere, but your best bet for finding gold are streams and rivers, since riverbeds are constantly tumbled by water. Also the moving water does something more than uncover new gravel, it also organizes material by density. Gold is heavy, almost twice as heavy as lead, so it will drop from the current first, then sand and gravel will cover it up. The material that covers over the gold is called "overburden."

To find gold, all you need is a gold pan and a shovel. The gold pan plays a huge role in your search. Panning looks easy, but maybe you've seen someone spackling drywall, fly-fishing, or playing a piano, it all looks easy for experts, but there is a technique to it. The densest material in the pan should leave the pan last. (Put ball bearings in to test your technique. If you're technique is sound, the ball bearing should be at the bottom of the pan after all the sand and gravel has gone. If the ball bearings come out while you pan, you need to adjust your technique.)

Once you find a spot to pan, shovel some of the riverbed into your pan — so that it's about a quarter full. Then cover the pan with water, tip it forward, so that the gravel/sand mixture is deepest where the bottom meets the side. Shake the pan back and forth — this is called "liquefaction," which is another way of letting water and movement suspend the material so that the denser substances fall to the bottom. Then the pan is dipped and lifted, letting the water gently carry away the lighter material. Repeat the liquefaction step, rinse, repeat. Keep panning until most of the material is gone and only the heaviest things remain.

Panning for gold is all about letting the gold sink to the bottom of the pan. A sluice can be used to help go though the debris. Too much water too fast, though, and most everything flows through and back into the river. And keep your eyes peeled for nuggets — gold prospecting is an exercise in perpetual optimism — before tossing the stuff in the screen back into the river. (Word to the Wise: Don't

Imperial Weight

Prospectors, as much as they would love to measure their gold findings in ounces, usually find it easier to speak in terms of pennyweight. A pennyweight equals 1/20 of an ounce. It was once the weight of an old British penny, but now it's more useful to think of it as 1.5 grams.

Thar's Gold in Them Thar Bedrooms

In 1923 a young boy named Brendon Thurston found a strange seven-pound rock while playing on a beach near his Tremont home on Mount Desert Island. It was heavy for its size. He put it in his closet and forgot about it. In 1939, sixteen years later, the boy's father found the rock while cleaning. He noticed yellow flakes around the rock. A New York firm evaluated the rock and found it contained five pounds of pure gold. Even at thirty-two dollars an ounce, that was real money in the bank in 1939.

toss back the discarded stuff where you are working because you don't want to keep going back through the same material over and over). Gold nuggets will lodge in the upper part of the sluice. Prospecting is about paying attention. If you run out of time, you can always take the sluice apart and take the "concentrates" home for panning on your own back porch.

And remember, the more material you go through, the more likely you are to find "some color." The most important part of your prospector's kit (no, it's not the sweat-stained hat and beard) is your gold pan. You could use a pie pan, but modern gold pans have ridges that help with the trapping of gold — and beginners need all the help they can get.

And always look for illuminated yellow: gold doesn't flash or sparkle, it glows. Generally speaking, the more material you look through, the more gold you will find! The same gold they buried King Tut in. The same gold that Black Beard crunched between his teeth. The same gleaming stuff that fills Fort Knox. ■

Gold Fever

In 1960, the town of Ogunquit, Maine, needed a new parking lot. The town dredged gravel from the river for the project. Someone thought they saw gold flakes in the gravel. The person got a gold pan and ended up finding a small nugget and about a quarter teaspoon of gold flakes. It only took a day and a half for news to spread (there were no blogs or Internet in the 1960s), attracting more than 2,500 prospectors who descended from all over the country to the parking lot gravel pile. Town officials panicked as the chaos around the gravel pile escalated. They called in the Army Corps of Engineers to quickly bulldoze the pile flat and pave it over.

11 The Ice Cometh

THESE DAYS, WE DON'T THINK THAT MUCH ABOUT ICE. Ice is like the Web: easy and free. Everybody, it seems, has an automatic icemaker in their freezers that shoots out ice, crushed or in cubes, with the simple touch of a button.

But it wasn't that long ago that we didn't have refrigeration. My great-grandmother was born in 1909 and still remembers getting ice delivered. And the icebox didn't plug-in to anything; it was just a box.

In the 1840s, the first blocks of ice arrived in England from the Wenham Lake Ice Company, which was located in Massachusetts. Each morning in the summer, the company put a three-hundred-pound block of ice in their store window. The people on the street were amazed, but it took another ten years for the average person to start using ice to keep their milk and meat from spoiling.

The Wenham Company produced less than ten thousand tons of ice each year at its peak, whereas almost a million tons of ice came from the Kennebec River here in Maine. Wehham made lake ice famous overseas, but Maine made lots more ice. It's all about marketing. Who would have thought you could market frozen lake water? It's not so silly. Now we market regular water, sell it in small bottles. It's all the rage.

In 1913, the first household refrigeration units for homes were invented. They didn't become common household items until much later, though. Refrigeration eventually killed the lake ice industry. So block ice was still an important feature in my grandmother's lifetime. Her family put blocks of ice in their ice-box on a daily basis.

Now the commercial market for lake ice is all but dead, but the tradition of harvesting ice still goes on at the Thompson Ice House in South Bristol, Maine.

Every February, on President's Day, hundreds of volunteers meet at the Thompson Ice House to do battle with ice blocks.

Ice Cutting Tools

An ice tong helped move the ice blocks

An ice saw cut the short sides of the ice blocks

A grapple or ice hook towed sheets of ice along channels and hauled blocks up the chute

A scoop net cleaned channels

A breaking off bar (similar to a crowbar) was used to detach sheets from the field of ice

A caulking bar filled grooves with chips to prevent flooding and freezing

A splitting chisel separated sheets into cakes

A bar chisel loosened and trimmed cakes of ice

A house bar separated small cakes of ice

A hook chisel split blocks and settled them on the elevator

They use the same tools that five generations cut ice blocks with from the pond right next door to the icehouse. The rookies use the hand-powered saws that look just like the old lumberjack cross-cut saws, to cut a grid pattern in the pond. The more experienced use an antique sled with a motor that chugs along, spinning a huge circular saw driven by a big flat belt.

The sled makes fast work of cutting out a grid of three hundred-pound ice blocks.

The goal is to never pick up the ice — and the volunteers don't.

The first ice blocks are cut in a long line leading up to the icehouse. These are the first ice blocks off the pond. This becomes an open canal for the rest of the ice blocks that people guide along with sharp-ended sticks to the ice house, while the grids of ice blocks get cut from the rest of the pond.

When an ice block reaches the end of the canal, a couple of people lower a sled down the icehouse ramp to the water level. It slides below the ice block and they haul the whole thing back up the icy ramp. Wet ice on ice, so there's not much friction here, but the ice workers still have to lift that weight, not just guide it along, like the people at the canal. Then the ice slides down to the one guy in the icehouse. And he has to deal with this sliding three hundred pounds of ice coming right at him. His job is to slide it into the proper spot.

The workers start cutting ice at about 9 a.m., by 2 p.m. it's all stacked in the ice house, as neat as dominos in a box. Next they cover the ice with sawdust. This keeps the ice blocks frozen through the summer — some blocks are sold as late as Labor Day.

And here is the really cool thing (excuse the pun): fishermen still buy small ice blocks from the Thompson Ice House for a dollar. The fishermen use this ice to keep their catch from spoiling while out on the ocean.

In 1922 a Model T cost $450. A refrigerator that very same year cost almost twice as much: $714.

For my great-grandmother, iceboxes were a way of life. Now most people I know don't even use an ice tray to make ice cubes. But that way of life can still be found in winter on a pond in South Bristol. ■

12 To Climb or Not to Climb Maine's Highest Mountain?

**IT'S EASY TO WRITE "CLIMB KATAHDIN,"
EASIER STILL TO SAY THE WORDS.** I wrote
them as an idea when I was thinking about this book: "Climb
Katahdin. It is 5,268 feet above sea level."

But those words tell nothing of what it feels like to actually
climb Katahdin. Like Mount Everest, no one climbs Katahdin by
accident.

Summers can go by like a high-speed freight train, thun-
dering into our lives and leaving us with the diminishing echoes
of things we might have done. But there, stuck to the side of my
computer was a sticky note, mocking me with its simplicity of
something that never got done. It read: Climb Katahdin.

The long, carefree days of summer had gone. But in their
place came fall and with it those gorgeous mountain-climbing
days. The bugs had disappeared. And the chances of heatstroke
had been replaced with an abundance of colorful trees.

The best time to climb Katahdin is fall and the best place to start once you've decided to hike Katahdin is with Baxter State Park's Web site.

Here are some nuts and bolts of what you need to know in order to begin your ascent:

You cannot just show up and climb this mountain. First you have to get to Baxter State Park. This alone can involve a substantial amount of driving. Even with the seventy-five-miles-per hour speed limit on I-95 north of Bangor, it's still about a three-hour drive from midcoast Maine. Also, Baxter closes on October 15. After the fifteenth you need full alpine climbing gear. The park rangers won't even let you in unless you show them your ice axes, crampons, and bundles of technical climbing rope.

One other important thing to remember when climbing Katahdin is that you will need most of the available daylight to reach the summit. So you need to arrive early. Really early, like 7:05 at the South Gate if you want to keep your parking reservation. You can drive up the night before and stay at one of the few hotels in Millinocket or you can drive up before and get a campground, like Big Moose Inn Cabins and Campground. A better option is to camp at the park itself, since you can get an earlier start. But campgrounds fill up even faster than parking reservations — the tenting spots were full weeks before I planned to climb the mountain.

And day hike is accurate. Officially it's a hike that must be climbed in a day; there are no other options. But the image of a day hike does not paint the proper picture.

The Native Americans saw mountains as hollow heights that held special powers that could range from evil to the humorous. So be prepared for the unexpected when hiking the "Greatest Mountain." For example, a surprise waited for me at the gate on my first trip to Katahdin. I got there at 6:30. More accurately, I pulled up to a line of stopped, bumper-to-bumper cars that disappeared out of sight around the corner. When I finally did move, I started seeing people driving out of the park, their faces wrecked by some tragic news. They were being turned back for not having a parking permit. So make sure you get your parking permit.

Just let me say that guidebooks and the people I talked to about climbing Katahdin never really painted the true picture of the experience of climbing Katahdin. First off, the mileage does not tell the whole story. There are hiking miles and then there are Katahdin miles. This is not a wandering "nature trail." All trails go directly up the mountain. The Hunt Trail climbs relentlessly from the beginning and will get your heart pounding hard. And then it gets steeper. But it's not just steep. There are thousands of opportunities to twist your ankle. The terrain is severe. The only way to get up and down is by foot. Motorcycles or four-wheelers can't get up to help you. If you can't walk on you own for any

Daypack Essentials

✔ **Water:** Always carry water (at least 2 quarts per person when climbing any of the mountains). Trailside springs are unreliable, as are any named springs denoted on maps of Katahdin.

✔ **Flashlight:** Plan hikes with the intention of finishing in daylight, but always carry a flashlight.

✔ **Extra food and clothing:** Candies, nuts, or dried fruit in addition to your lunch and liquids. Also wool/pile shirt and/or sweater, hat, extra socks, and raingear.

✔ **Sturdy footwear:** Trails are rocky and footing is difficult. For your safety, be sure footwear is adequate. Tennis shoes are not suitable for mountain climbing.

✔ **First aid:** Supplies, such as Band-Aids, ace bandages, and moleskin, to take care of you and those hiking in your group. Most common first aid problem: Blisters!

✔ **Map/guide book:** Know your route; plan alternatives for bad weather.

✔ **Other suggestions:** Compass, matches, foil emergency blanket, whistle, parachute cord, knife, pack repair kit.

reason, you will have to be carried out on a litter by rangers. And it won't be a fun ride. And you can't call time out or call in for a replacement. It's you and the peak, mountain man! This is the kind of thing that Ernest Hemingway meant when he said: "There are only three sports: bullfighting, motor racing, and mountaineering; all the rest are merely games."

Katahdin is not a game. It's real. And its beauty lies in knowing this. The mountain changes how you think about yourself and about nature. All the bravado melts away with the first mile and your pounding heart. You're sweat-soaked and chilled. You plod on, feeling overdressed and underdressed at the same time. Everything you need is strapped to your back. You have to stop every hour to eat, to stay ahead of any hunger/energy/thirst issues. Sometimes birches that stand next to big boulders serve as handholds; bark that has been polished smooth by thousands of hands. You can feel the ghosts of others climbers through the silky-worn spots on the trees. There is a comforting energy from touching them. A refueling, much like the beef jerky and Little Debbie pies.

This hike is some of the roughest terrain you'll ever hike. Nearly every step is another rock, another step up. Like a staircase with no pattern. But the most memorable thing about Katahdin is its ruggedness. Even when you make it to the peak, the wind buffets you, unchallenged and powerful. Katahdin is the real deal. It has claimed nineteen lives since 1963, mostly due to exposure to weather and falls from the Knife Edge due to high winds.

Nobody will grab you by the shoulders and look deep into your eyes before you attempt your climb of Maine's highest peak. This can be both refreshing and frightening at the same time. But all you have to do is read *Lost on a Mountain in Maine*, Donn Fendler's cautionary tale about his nine days and nights lost on the mountain, to realize that the mountain is a treacherous place, but also a wild and wonderful one, too.

At the trailhead to Katahdin Stream there is information about how to properly poop in the woods. There's also a photograph of smiling people with hair standing on end with a caption saying that moments later a person, only a couple feet away, was struck by a bolt of lightening.

You don't want to be struck by lightening on your climb to Katahdin. But you can't help being struck by its majestic beauty. ■

Katahdin Trails

- ✤ Cathedral Trail is so steep, it's not recommended for descending since it passes a series of three jutting rock formations — the Cathedrals. It's the shortest route between Chimney Pond and the summit. The trek is less than two miles and is very vertical.

- ✤ Chimney Pond Trail has jaw-dropping views of Katahdin's great wall, and the campground here allows hikers to rest here and make their one-day hike into two. The trail is 3.3 miles long and not that strenuous.

- ✤ Dudley Trail is a 1.4 mile trail that leaves Chimney Pond and makes a direct climb up to Pamola Peak, which is very exposed.

- ✤ Helon Taylor Trail is 3.2 miles long and takes hikers from Roaring Brook Campground to Keep Ridge to Pamola Peak. It's a rugged climb and then there is the Knife Edge when you're done.

- ✤ Hunt Trail is the last 2.5 miles of the Appalachian Trail and leaves from Katahdin Stream Campground and is loved by hikers due to its varied terrain.

- ✤ Knife Edge is perhaps the most dangerous mile of hiking on the mountain, this infamous hike is only three feet wide in places, with a thousand-foot drop on either side. It can be especially precarious on windy days.

- ✤ Northwest Basin Trail is an 8.3 mile pathway that takes trekkers into the Northwest Basin, home of Davis Pond and an area that is considered of mystical beauty.

- ✤ Saddle Trail is a 2.2 mile trek that leaves from Chimney Pond and is considered the most gradual approach to the summit. But it's not without its challenges.

- ✤ Abol Trail is a perfect day hike at 7.6 miles round-trip. It's very steep, but it's also the shortest trip to Baxter Peak, and the views are stunning.

13 Stalking Night Crawlers

STALKING NIGHT CRAWLERS MIGHT SEEM LIKE A JOKE. There appears to be no sport in digging up slow worms and plopping them into a can.

Think again! Stalking for night crawlers will soon get you hooked.

First it helps if it has rained during the day, since this will make the crawlers crawl. They crawl out onto the grass because their holes are waterlogged and they wriggle out in the safety of darkness, thinking all predators are gone.

Ha!

Even in a dry spell you can get those crawlers out. Just give the lawn a good soaking with a sprinkler.

But to catch those night crawlers, you're going to need stealth. You need to move softly. Worms are very sensitive to vibrations. Just a slight rustle in the grass, and they're gone. These lightning-fast worms can also sense bright light. (I know, they don't have eyes, but they know when a beam of light hits them.) If you must stalk with a flashlight, make sure not to direct the beam at them. Instead, let your eyes acclimate to the darkness. A headlamp works best since then you have both hands free for nabbing and for holding your container. I found a wonderful little lamp that clips to the brim of my baseball hat, and it has several different light intensities, the lower the beam, the better.

But what's all this talk about worms being fast?

It's true. A night crawler stretched out on the dewy night grass disappears in an instant if you make one wrong move.

Now it's time for the hunt to begin! First allow your eyes to adjust to the dark. Also be sure to pick a night with no thunder or heavy wind or rain. (Remember, night crawlers are sensitive things.) And short grass makes the hunting easier. (Hint: Cut the grass if it's long.)

After your eyes adjust, scan the area with your flashlight for night crawler activity. Keep an eye open for the lower areas where more rain collects, a place where water drains and concentrates.

Take your time. Bask in the solitude of evening and your quiet hunt.

Your eyes will get used to seeing the worms after a while.

Now your image of the common earthworm is probably of a slow, wriggling annelid that you've dug up in the garden or else you've spotted a sluggish and dying one in a puddle.

At night, it's different. At night they are big and they are fast. Night crawlers at night are a special breed. And they always seem to have one end still in the hole. Grab that end in the hole! Grab with a blinding but gentle speed. Worms snap in two, so don't use brute force. Be gentle with your prey. Once you have ahold of the worm, be still. Pull gently only when the worm relaxes. If he tenses up, stop pulling and wait. Take your time.

Worms coat themselves in an incredibly slippery slime. This makes it hard to get a good grip. So carry a bag of sawdust with you and dip your grabbing hand into it frequently. No more slippery worm trouble. And soon your can will be overflowing with night crawlers.

If there's a lesson to hunting night crawlers it's this: Don't ever let a worm outsmart you. And even if one does, go back and hunt it again! ▬

14 Gone Fishing

LIGHT TACKLE IS ALL YOU NEED FOR MACK-EREL FISHING. I usually start with a simple mackerel jig, which is nothing more than a bare hook with a shiny metal head. It doesn't look fancy enough to catch anything, but it works.

I brought my son along, and on his first cast something hit his lure and ran. The sun glared off the glassy waves. His fishing pole danced and throbbed. His line ripped left and right in the calm water. Then we saw it, a silver flashing like a distorted chrome dagger flying through the water.

Mackerel!

For a small fish, mackerel really put up a good fight.

I often cut up the first mackerel and use it for bait. Next I switch to a bare hook. Sometimes I use a bobber, to keep the bait near the top, or a sinker a couple of feet from the hook to let the bait drift along the bottom, letting the current move it back and forth.

Of course, the best method is what actually works. It always pays to keep an eye on the setup of the person who catches the most fish. They are obviously doing something right. If they are on the ocean side; you go to the ocean side. If they fish the bot-

A guy at Johnson's Sporting Goods taught me all I needed to know about using a jig: "Throw it out there. Haul it. Reel it. Let it sink a little. Haul it...."

53

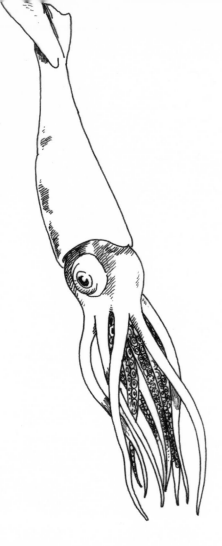

tom; you fish the bottom. And if the fish start running, keep at it. A run can drop off to nothing in an instant. A school of stripers, or a seal, can stop the feeding frenzy of mackerel faster than switching off a light.

Some people catch mackerel to use as bait — stripers love mackerel. Others catch mackerel to eat. A mackerel makes a tasty meal. But if you want to enjoy your mackerel, keep in mind that freshness counts. And "fresh" doesn't mean dead fish sitting in a plastic shopping bag on a piece of hot granite while the August sun beats on it for hours. Mackerel spoil fast and they lose their tastiness even faster, so if you want the best tasting meal, take a small cooler full of ice with you.

I like to gut the catch right on the water since this keeps the meat fresher longer.

Catch it. Clean it. Eat it. My simple rule to fishing.

Night Angling for Squid

Nighttime is the best time to catch squid. So when the tide rolls in on a warm August evening, head to the harbor and catch some squid. Light tackle is all you need. And it's a quiet activity, conducive to talk and laugher. Plus seven dollars will get you a glow-in-the-dark torpedo-like lure — the sole admission price to Squidland.

Squid don't put up a huge fight. Their "bite" is soft, subtle, so the angler needs to keep a light touch on the line. When a squid grabs the lure — which has a couple rows of needle-sharp hooks without barbs — with its tentacles, it feels the hooks snag, and it reacts by grabbing with more tentacles.

Some anglers recommend fishing for squid on the incoming tide. Some say fish at night to appeal to the nocturnal tendency of squid. What I've found is that squid run when they run. And if you have your jig in the water when they run, you will catch some "squirts," as they are called.

Squid have a soft feel when they grab the lure, so there's no need to jerk the pole. Mild pressure is the key, because squid grab with delicate tentacles. Jerk too hard and you will lose you catch. A gentle, firm pressure works best.

When hauled from the water, a squid's propulsion system gushes the last of the seawater out as they encounter air. They shoot this last water out in an effort to jet away from danger. They also make all kinds of grunting noises as they try to reload with seawater. They also have a defense mechanism: they "ink." So don't wear your favorite Bean Boots if you go squid fishing. But if you get ink on your hands and clothes, it's water-soluble and washes out if you act before it dries. Squid shoot ink in a last bid not to become calamari or bait.

Squid Fishing Techniques

The chances of catching squid are more favorable during high tide on a cloudy or rainy night. These conditions give the shore water the depth that squid like as well as a setting in which the artificial light is most noticeable.

Sometimes a single lure works best; sometimes multiple lures (up to four) are better. By putting lures of different sizes and colors on the line, you can test which type works best to attract squid. You should also experiment with the arrangement of lures. Sometimes putting the same lures in a different order makes a big difference.

> ## Squid Lore
> ✔ Fish at night.
> ✔ Find a place to fish with a big streetlight. The light attracts squid.
> ✔ Try different depths.
> ✔ Try different color lures.
> ✔ Keep your jig moving at all times.
> ✔ Set the hook gently when you feel the slightest pull on your line.
> ✔ Use a split-shot sinker just in front of the jig.
> ✔ Rumors have it that big squid runs happen somewhere around mid-August.
> ✔ Getting a squid off the line involves grabbing the head of the jig and tipping it upside down. Then the squid will slide off a barbless hook. Don't make the mistake of slowly lowering the squid into the bucket before releasing it; the squid will just grab hold of the plastic bucket. And don't fill the bucket with water — the squid will just "ink up" the water and you won't be able to count your catch.

Cleaning Squid

✔ Cut the squid in half just below the eyes

✔ Find the small black beak and remove with your fingers

✔ Wash the tentacles in cold water and place in a bowl

✔ Make a second cut above the eyes. Discard the eyes

✔ Cut off the two suckers that hang from the tentacle area (chickens seem to really like these parts)

✔ Take a finger and thrust it into the upper section of the squid, called the tube.

✔ Run your finger around to separate all the visceral mass, ink sack, and the plastic-looking feather bone

✔ Rinse again

If using a single lure, cast it out some distance and allow it to sink to where squid are lurking. Then retrieve it with a series of steady jerks or "jigs." If using multiple lures, simply lower them down to a chosen depth in lighted water. Then slowly raise them up and down, over and over. Squid hole up in dark water around well-lit areas then lunge into the brighter arena when they see something that looks edible. Then they deftly wrap their tentacles around their prey.

When a slight change is felt in your rod, jerk it upward, which immediately sets the hooks. Then keep a steady upward motion as you reel or lift the catch to the surface. Remember: the hooks on squid jigs are barbless, so most of the time the squid isn't really hooked, just entwined in the prongs, so any slack in the line will lose the catch.

Every day in Maine, there are two high tides and two low tides. Unfortunately, this has lead many people to think there are two Maines: Portland and the rest of the state.

If you are going to go squid fishing, you need to pay attention to the tide and keep a local tide chart handy. If you plan to fish a midnight high tide on a Saturday, you will need to know the high tide on Sunday will be an hour later. Later in the week, and the high tide happens just as the sun is rising. There are many factors that affect tides, but the biggest is the moon. As the Earth spins, the gravitational force from the moon pulls on the Earth, but the moon's most dramatic effect is on large bodies of water, like our oceans. When the sun and moon are both on the same side of the Earth, the sun contributes some gravitational force that combines with the moon's pull. When this happens, we have a spring tide, which is the strongest of all tides. Spring tides happen around the full moon and the new moon. Neap tides occur between the full and new moon — when the moon is quartered to the sun and the two forces cancel each other a bit, making tides that are not as extreme as the spring tide.

Also take a bucket. A dry-wall-type bucket seems most popular. But its five-gallon capacity has, so far, been overly optimistic for me. Although I've heard talk of a "big run," a mid-August frenzy where a lucky fisherman can fill a five-gallon bucket with squid. Also once you plop a squid into the bucket, it's fun to watch it start changing colors, running from almost colorless to red to almost black, trying to find a color that will get it out of the bucket.

No chance. It's coming home with you for calamari. ∎

Calamari: Bon Appetite!

Sprinkle cleaned squid (see "Cleaning Squid") with sea salt and a touch of black bean sauce or fresh chilies

Sauté in oil

Toss on a hot grill for 3 to 4 minutes, no more (too long will toughen the squid)

Serve with a tomato, cucumber, and basil salad. And uncork a chilled bottle of white wine

Or deep fry squid in a simple batter of flour, water, salt, and pepper. Delicious!

Note: *Some people like to skin the squid, others like it left on. If you want the skin off, you can scrape a small piece with a fingernail or the back of a knife and peel it off like you're peeling a sticker.*

15 Bike the Down East Sunrise Trail

Other Good Cycling Trails

Maine Huts and Trails network in Kingfield

Carriage Roads in Acadia National Park
St. John Valley Heritage Trail

Aroostook Valley Trail

Bangor and Aroostook Trail

Kennebec Valley Trail

Portland Area Trails

Eastern Trail in Southern Maine

NEARLY EVERYONE HAS A BICYCLE OR EVEN TWO IN THEIR GARAGE. GIVEN A BICYCLE, AND SOME SIMPLE GEAR, PLUS SOME TIME AND DETERMINATION, A PERSON CAN EXPLORE THE BYWAYS AND THE HIGHWAYS OF MAINE ON TWO WHEELS. Not just around the neighborhood, either, but as far as you want to go — think up to the County or even way Down East.

Maine is an ideal state for cycling. Recent reports rank the state tenth nationally in the number of people who bike to work. Plus Maine has the most effective advocacy group in the county, the Bicycle Coalition of Maine, which rigorously promotes bicycling as an easy, safe, and popular sport.

And the Down East Sunrise Trail is a perfect place to start. This multi-use corridor (you can walk, cycle, snowmobile, cross-country-ski, and ATV) stretches from Washington Junction in Hancock County to Ayers Junction Down East, some eighty-five, car-free miles long. The Sunrise Trail is part of a route called the Green Way that stretches from Key West, Florida, the southernmost point in the continental U.S., all the way to the Canadian border.

My son and I wanted to set off on bikes for an overnight ride.

I'm no novice to cycling. In the mid-1980s, I put five thousand miles on a bicycle ride from North Carolina to Florida and back, then to New Orleans, through Texas to New Mexico. In 2008, I completed the longest self-supported off-road bicycle race in the world. It took me twenty-nine days to cover the 2,700 miles from Banff, Alberta, down dirt trails through the Rocky Mountains to the Mexican border. Our trip would be a little different in scale but similar in spirit.

We took as much gear as would fit in a medium-size car trunk for our overnight ride along the Down East Sunrise Trail. We packed a lot of water; something very important under the blazing sun as refill sites are many miles apart. We also packed some of my favorite long-distance bicycle foods: Hostess pies.

Packed, we headed east for our cycling adventure.

The Sunrise Trail is a former railway bed so it avoids any steep grades. The smooth surface of crushed gravel really allows for a steady roll; it doesn't require a hardcore mountain bike. The grades are so gentle, you could easily do it with a single-speed bike. It's not a grueling cycle, but it's a long one if you do the whole eighty-five miles, so you should definitely pace yourself and plan your trip out — like where to stay the night, since services are extremely limited along the trail and there are surprisingly few flat places to pitch a tent.

The trail itself winds through sparse countryside of dense brush and close, spindly trees. At times, it can feel a bit desolate, but the freedom from cars and trucks creates a real sense of peace and allows for an enjoyable, worry-free ride. For the forty miles we covered, the terrain didn't change much, except for crossing the occasional stream and the Narraguagus River in Cherryfield.

If we had decided on cycling the whole of the trail, I'm sure with an extra push we could have finished on the following day. Even a kid can go a long way on this smooth trail with very little worries.

At the end of our ride, both my son and I could talk of nothing but pizza in Harrington. It almost started to sound like some mystical place. The pizza joint even pointed us to a campground on the ocean that was two miles away. We arrived and set up our tent just as the sun was setting, casting an orange glow over the silence of evening.

We drifted off to sleep in our warm sleeping bags as the smell of the ocean descended with the dew on our tent. ∎

16 Splitting Fire-Wood Like a Lumberjack

THE NUMBER OF HOUSEHOLDS USING WOOD AS THEIR PRIMARY HEATING SOURCE NEARLY DOUBLED IN MAINE FROM 2000 TO 2010. No wonder we see so many people splitting firewood.

The first step to having wood is to cut the tree. Then chainsaw it to length. Then split it.

The Splitting

Put the chainsawed wood on its end, on a chopping block if possible. If not, the ground will do. Now place yourself in such a way that when you swing the axe with straight arms, the blade hits the wood. Make sure there's no one around and nothing you want damaged nearby. Stand with your legs a little apart, pull the axe straight back over your head, and swing it straight forward. As you build up speed, the momentum and weight of the ax will do all the work — not your brute strength.

Try to hit the same place every time. You will get the axe stuck in the wood many times and have to wrestle it out, but eventually the wood will split. When it starts to, make a few gentle hits in the crack to separate the wood fibers still connecting the pieces together.

I've found there's no better alone time for solving problems than when you're splitting wood. ■

What You Need

A maul or axe. A maul is heavier and has a wider head than an axe, but an ax can work just as well for smaller wood-splitting jobs. Also, remember, you're not cutting wood or even chopping it: you're *splitting* wood. So that axe doesn't even need to be that sharp.

Wood. Seasoned wood splits better. If the wood has nails in it, don't bother. It's not worth damaging your axe or losing an eye when that nail flies. And if the wood's got a knot in it, skip it, especially if it's green.

17 11 Books Every Mainer Should Read

The Next Bend in the River by C.J. Stevens

C.J. Stevens takes you on a gold-rush ride in Maine — its past and its present. He wonderfully introduces the characters that live and prospect on the Swift River. This book explores Stevens' love for a river, as well as all the sifting and digging for that elusive gold. It also chronicles his obsession for gold: a road trip for the precious metal that destroys his car and cleans out his bank account looking for those nuggets.

Lost on a Mountain in Maine by Donn Fendler

This is a short, true story about a boy lost on Mount Katahdin. Donn Fendler is still alive and still goes to schools to tell his story about being lost for nine days on Maine's legendary mountain. It's a page-turner, and a must-read if you are going to hike Katahdin.

We Took to the Woods by Louise Dickinson Rich

Louise Dickinson Rich will take you back into the 1940s woods of Maine. Louise and her husband heat with wood. They tinker with engines because there is no one else to do the tinkering. They have a phone that works every now and then when the line hasn't been snapped by fallen trees. Louise and her husband don't ever need to go looking for adventure: it always seems to find them. Louise's writing rings so true for our contemporary need for stories of adventure that it continues to sell more than a thousand copies a year.

The Maine Atlas and Gazetteer by DeLorme

Simply put: You need this map! Even if you have a GPS, get a *Gazetteer*. If it rides with you everywhere, eventually its tattered corners and smudged pages will tell the many stories of your trips and adventures around Maine — the way only a real map can.

The Terrible Hours: The Greatest Submarine Rescue in History by Peter Maas

In 1939, the USS *Squalus* went down on her maiden voyage just off the coast of Maine. This is the story of what happened as the terrible hours ticked away. As the oxygen ran low below in the darkness of the sub, the people on the surface used Charles "Swede" Momsen's equipment to try to save the thirty-three sailors trapped 243 feet below the cold Atlantic.

The Hungry Ocean: A Swordboat Captain's Journey by Linda Greenlaw

Find out where storms go when they go "safely out to sea," as the TV weathermen are so fond of saying. They go out into the Atlantic, where the successful fisherman Linda Greenlaw not only makes her living, but also spends most of her time. Go "safely out to sea" with a crew of tough men who work in all weather and who look to Greenlaw when the going gets tough.

The Sign of the Beaver by Elizabeth George Speare

The year is 1768. Twelve-year-old Matt and his father head north to Maine to build a cabin and settle, leaving the rest of the family behind. They get a crop planted and a cabin built. Matt's father leaves him with a hunting rifle and his prized watch, telling him he will return in about seven weeks with his mother and new baby sister. Matt runs out of food, encounters bears and angry bees. He finds himself in trouble and alone when he meets up with his greatest fear, the Indians.

Charlotte's Web by E.B. White

Maybe you've seen the cartoon and feel like you know the story. Think again. White's writing is clear and simple, his voice strong. Even if you know the story, you haven't experienced E.B. White until you've read this book. Start with *Charlotte's Web* and then move on to the rest of his work. You'll not be disappointed. Although you might cry a little.

Following Fake Man by Barbara Ware Holmes

Homer Winthrop thinks he's never been in Maine before, but he has; when he was a baby and his father was still alive. While visiting from Boston, Homer makes friends with a boy named Roger and they begin to follow a secretive man who takes a strange cardboard box out to Owl Island every day. The boys follow him out to a cabin, intent on solving the mystery of the fake man and soon discover more than they expected — about who the mysterious man is and about Homer Winthrop's father, who died when Homer was just two years old.

The Lobster War by Trevor Wood

Sixteen-year-old Dain's father died when he fell overboard while lobster fishing. Dain's mother wants him to go to college, but Dain wants to be like his father. In his first summer lobstering, he starts to notice his traps disappearing. He suspects Roger, the most feared character in town, of stealing his traps. Tough decisions await Dain in a storm when he finds the trap thieves in trouble.

The Mostly True Adventures of Homer P. Figg
by Rodman Philbrick

Homer P. Figg's mother dies in 1863 as the Civil War rages on. After his mother's death, Homer finds himself in Pine Swamp, Maine, in the custody of his Uncle Squinton Leach. Homer runs away to search for his brother, who was sold to the army by his mean uncle. Homer meets a wide range of characters, from foolish to dangerous, in his search for his brother. ■

18 How to Build a Rustic Shelter

MAINE IS KNOWN FOR ITS HISTORIC FORTS, LIKE FORT WESTERN IN AUGUSTA, BUILT IN 1754 BY THE PLYMOUTH COMPANY TO PROTECT THE NEW WORLD SETTLERS FROM FRENCH AND NATIVE AMERICAN ATTACKS. There are twenty-seven forts in Maine, scattered across the state from Kittery to Eastport to Fort Kent.

Don't worry, this fort is much simpler to build than those mighty fortresses. In fact, you don't even need lumber to build this one. You can build it from materials you find in the woods. And you can make your fort for free, and when you are done, it will simply collapse back into the landscape, so it's environmentally safe.

This fort is based on a Wabanaki shelter; a skeletal frame of saplings, bent into arches, then covered with birch bark that is stitched together. Young maples are the ideal saplings for this because in order to survive, they go straight for the sky. They don't mess around with getting fat. They grow long and thin.

So take along your pruning saw and cut a bunch of saplings that are similar in length and diameter. You want to make

Under Thatch

You can also use tall grasses as a covering, but make sure your horizontal bands are close enough together so that when you fold your grass in half, you still have plenty of overlap with the next grass layer. If done correctly, it should look like a thatched roof. The disadvantage to thatching is the amount of work it will take to cut and lash all that grass to your hut.

your dome eight to ten feet in diameter. Next, tie two saplings together to form an "X". Then bend both saplings into an arch and then jamb their ends into the ground, keeping the sides as vertical as you can — this will give you more room inside. Keep adding arches, until you split the space into two. This will give you a nice dome-shaped structure.

After you have enough arches, it's time to weave in the horizontal bands. These should be smaller in diameter, and flexible sticks. They get threaded through the arches, alternating between every other one in a basket-weave pattern.

In order to decide how close these bands need to be, you need to know what material you want to use to cover your fort. The easiest material is leaves. If you use leaves, your bands need to be closer together; no bigger than a hand's width apart.

Next, gather a huge stack of leaves — the bigger the better. Start stuffing all the holes in your fort with handfuls of leaves. Then keep piling them on. The more leaves, the warmer your hut will be — it will also repel all but a heavy rain. Plus your fort will now blend into the woods, which is very cool.

Now add a couple mats and some sleeping bags, and you've got a fine fort, worthy of the early settlers. ■

19 How to Survive a Fall Through Ice

NOBODY WANTS TO FALL THROUGH ICE. BUT THEN NOBODY WANTS TO GET A SPEEDING TICKET. Sometimes, though, events happen to us that are out of our control. But there are a few simple precautions you can take to avoid an accident that can so quickly turn into a perilous life and death struggle.

1. Do Not Drown. This might seem stupid and obvious, but the involuntary gasping, caused by the frigid water shocking your system, is hard to control. Try to keep your head above water during the gasping phase. You will gasp, this is nearly unavoidable, but do everything you can to keep your head above water. You will feel scared, personally wronged. It will be uncomfortable, but the gasping will pass. This phase can last up to a minute. It's called "cold shock."

2. Go Back From Where You Came. Why? Because the ice where you came from is strong enough to hold you. The ice in front of you doesn't come with the same guarantee. Plus you have more time than you think. This is a survival game, so use

> ### Important Point
> If someone goes through the ice, don't run out after them. That will put two people into danger. If you have a cellphone, call for help. Next, look around for a rope to throw, a ladder you can slide to them, or a long stick so you can pull them out from a distance. If you throw a rope, put a loop in it so the person can get it around his or her body, or at least put his or her arm through it.

Ice Brawns

Generally speaking, it takes four inches of ice to safely support an average person on their feet. But all ice is not equal. Black ice is the strongest. It's the kind of ice that you can see through. Snow ice is weaker and needs to be thicker in order to support your weight. A spring or current can erode ice in spots. Just because the ice is thick in one spot doesn't mean that it will hold you.

your time wisely. Panic will only cause you to run out of strength faster. Cold water robs your strength fast and it will take away your mental clarity. Be aware of this. Know that if you have been in cold water for more than ten minutes, your muscles will lose strength to do simple tasks and your judgment will begin to fail, use this knowledge to your advantage. Keep things simple. Your survival depends on heading back to where you know the ice will support you and allow you to climb out.

3 Climbing Out. Keep your body as horizontal as possible, basically in the swimming position, instead of the treading-water position as you climb out. Do this by kicking your feet at the same time that you use your arms and hands to climb out. If you make it onto the ice, stay on your belly. You want as much of your body in contact with the ice as possible. If you lay on your belly, much thinner ice will support your body than if you stand

Hypothermia

The thing to remember is that it takes a long time to die from hypothermia, the loss of your core body temperature, but not so long for your muscles to lose strength and for you to slip under the water and drown. Let's say you fall through the ice and that it takes you ten minutes to get out. At this point, your skin has lost the ability to feel the cold and you probably feel weak. But you've stopped shivering and you've only lost a half degree of your core temperature. That doesn't sound like much, but it is. When the outside of you body starts to warm back up, your core temperature will drop again — as much as one more degree. Then your body will start to shiver uncontrollably, this is not really comfortable or fun, but it's really a good sign. It means you are on your way back to your normal temperature. Your body wants to survive. When it starts cooling off, it starts limiting blood, and therefore heat, to all secondary systems. I know we don't want to think of arms and legs as secondary, but your body, when it goes into emergency lockdown, wants to keep the heat and oxygen to vital organs (brain, liver, kidneys, etc.). When the heat starts coming back to the outside of your body, your body cancels the emergency signal and starts sending blood to your arms and legs, pulling heat from your core to help get the other systems warm again.

Just for the Experience

It was a simple plan formed in a warm living room in winter where brave talk comes easy. I decided I would take a cold-water plunge in order to find out what frigid January water feels like. I don't recommend this exercise to any of my readers, it was a foolish, albeit enlightening, experience that taught me one thing: Don't ever fall into icy water!

Ice chips danced as my two-cycle chainsaw smoked and screamed in the frozen air. I had cut a six-foot-wide circle of open water, surrounded by big broken teeth of ice. The water shimmered with the iridescent colors of chainsaw oil and smoke.

Now the moment of truth came. I peeled off my Carhartt overalls and big Sorrel boots and jumped into the icy water.

My diaphragm immediately spasmed, making strange gasping sounds that were beyond my control.

Immersion in water that is just a degree or two above freezing knocks all the bravado out of a person. My first reaction was to blurt out about how cold the water is; I also had a strong urge to get out of the water.

After totally immersing, I pulled myself out, a process very similar to hauling yourself out of a concrete swimming pool. And I remember thinking, if I had fallen through the ice, the ice around me would not support my weight like this two-foot-thick stuff, but this thought flew out of my mind quickly as I had a new, inexplicable, and irrepressible urge to run around in circles on the ice, my bare feet smacking away like frozen boards.

And then a strange thing happened. I stopped running in circles and really wanted to get back in. I eased back into the dark oily water, but this time the water enveloped me with welcoming warmth. I wasn't hypothermic. The water was just warmer than the air.

Eventually my shield of warmth faltered as the reality of the cold settled in. The frigid air and freezing water had taken its toll. I was getting cold.

Water steals body heat twenty to twenty-five times faster than air. That is why staying dry is so important to staying warm.

After my brisk swim, my body felt like I had chugged a couple quarts of coffee, a six-pack of cola, and maybe a few military specification Red Bulls. The super awareness and hyperactivity carried on late into the evening. I guess my body was on alert, trying to avoid another dip in cold water.

up. This same reasoning applies to why people put a ladder on the ice; it distributes your body weight over a large surface of ice.

◀ If You Can't Climb Out. You still have an option. Get your arms on the ice, lay them flat, and don't move. You are trying to get your arms to freeze to the ice. This sounds morbid, but if you lose consciousness, or just don't have any more strength, if your arms freeze to the ice, this could give rescuers another half hour to forty-five minutes to get to you. ■

20 Making Fire: Getting in Touch with Your Inner Caveman

YOU MAY ASK, WHY BOTHER MAKING FIRE IN A WORLD FULL OF MATCHES AND LIGHTERS? It would be a very odd situation in our modern age if we needed to make our own fire. But making fire puts us in touch with the original creators from our distant human past. When something smolders and bursts into flames before you, you own the same knowledge that started early humans on the path to civilization. Without fire, well, it's almost impossible to say what would have happened. But one thing is certain: there would have been no automobiles, Gortex, or penicillin.

So make fire using one of these methods and you will share the magic that the first humans felt when they produced a flame.

Friction Method

You might be skeptical about making fire with a stick and a shoelace, but it works. This is also one of the more finicky and physically tiring ways of making fire, but the satisfaction of starting a fire with a string and a couple pieces of wood makes the whole process worthwhile:

1 Look for a short, straight, sturdy twig about six inches long, gather kindling, a flat length of wood (I used a dry cedar board about ¾ inches thick, but any low-density wood, like white pine will work), a curved branch (about as long as your arm), and a stone with a round depression in it.

2 Remove one of your shoelaces and tie it tightly to both ends of the curved stick. Now you've made what is called a bow drill.

3 Loop the straight twig into the string of the bow drill.

4 Place the bottom of the straight twig firmly against the flat piece of wood and hold the stone on top of the twig's other end with your off hand.

5 Draw the bow back and forth, making the twig spin in place. Start out slowly to make sure nothing comes loose and then gradually speed up.

Making Char Cloth

Char cloth is easy to make, but make sure to do it outside, since it is a stinky, smoky process.

✔ Poke a small pinhole into the top of the can (an Altoids tin works well).

✔ Collect cotton rags and cut the material so it fits inside your tin.

✔ Do just two or three layers of cloth at a time. Too much cloth and the heat won't be able to get to all the material evenly.

✔ Apply heat directly to the tin (I cooked mine on the grill so I could get under it with a flame. You could also use a campfire or a camp stove. I used a propane torch and that worked well, too.) You should wait until you see a thin jet of smoke shooting out of the pinhole. When the smoke jet stops altogether, the char cloth is done.

✔ Let the whole thing cool.

6 Place kindling all around the spinning twig and continue to draw the bow back and forth until sparks begin to jump and land on the kindling.

7 Blow on the kindling lightly to get the sparks to catch fire. When this happens, start feeding the flame until the fire spreads to the piece of wood under the kindling. And, voila, fire!

Note: If the shoelace slips, tighten it on the bow. If the stick jumps out of the bow, you need to get your left foot closer to the stick and get your rock tighter against your shin. If it's not tight against your shin, you will have trouble holding your rock hand still as you go back and forth with the bow.

Magnifying Glass

Who doesn't remember as a child trying to make fire with a magnifying glass? It seems that starting a fire with a magnifying glass should be easy. But that's not been my experience. This is because the fuel (normally paper) burns away too quickly before it gathers enough heat to burst into flames.

An easier way is to use char cloth (see "Making Char Cloth" sidebar). It can help with the very first stages of a fire. It doesn't burn with a flame, but with an ember. Once you have an ember, place it in a timber bundle and blow and you will have a flame that you can then transfer to small twigs.

Char cloth ignites quickly, but since it does not make a flame, it may be hard to tell by looking at it if it has ignited or not. If you blow on it, an orange glow will tell you it's burning.

Ice and Fire

Making fire from frozen water. Are you crazy? At first it doesn't seem to make any sense, it just seems to go against everything we know about fire and ice. But if you freeze water into ice and then shape it into a lens, you can use it to focus the sun's rays into an intense beam.

To do this you will need crystal-clear ice. If you just freeze tap water, you will get cloudy ice. Filtered water works best. Next, boil the water, not once, but twice. (The whole point of boiling is to get ride of the air bubbles that are trapped in water.) Let it cool between boilings. Then slowly pour the water through a coffee filter into a plastic container, like a quart yogurt holder. Tip the container on its side when you pour to avoid trapping more air in the water. Let it cool to room temperature and then put the container, making sure it's level, into the freezer. After the water has frozen, pop it out of the container. If it's not clear, start again. It has to be clear.

You will now need to shape the ice with a sharp knife. Hold onto the ice with a dishtowel. You must exercise extreme caution when shaping your lens. Make sure you always carve with the blade angled away from you, so that if the blade does slip off, it can't hurt you. The goal of the carving is to dome the top, about a quarter to a half inch. Then do the same to the bottom.

Then comes the fun part — you need to smooth the lens. Use your warm hand to rub it into shape. Polish both sides like this.

Now you need sun. Use the ice as you would a magnifying glass. The shape of your lens will dictate the focal length. The best way to do this is by eye. You want to turn the lens to the sun to get the roundest beam, then move the lens in or out to focus the beam to the smallest dot.

Use it on a piece of char cloth and you'll soon have a campfire going.

Moxie Fire

Yes, the state's official and curious-tasting soft drink is not only good for you, it can also help you start a fire. And because this is Maine, it has to be Moxie, not Coke or Pepsi.

1 Drink the Moxie first....

2 Take toothpaste and polish the bottom of the soda can. You can polish it any way you want. Some people use very fine steel wool or very fine sandpaper. But the goal is to polish it until you can see your face in it.

3 Now point the bottom of the can *directly* at the sun. Alignment is important here, if you are off, the beam will not focus in the center. The focus length, where the beam will burn, should be somewhere between a half and one inch from the bottom of the can. To see the where the focus is, take a narrow piece of paper and extend it over the center (wide paper will block incoming rays). If the bottom of the can is pointed directly at the sun, the focused beam should be in the center. Move the paper in and out until the beam is the smallest. Just when it gets small, it should burn through.

4 Put a small piece of char cloth on a toothpick. Hold it in the focus area. You should get an ember soon. ◼

21 Go-Cart Racing

AH, THE IDYLLIC PASTIME OF GO-CART RACING IN MAINE.

Maybe you have a mental picture when it comes to go-carts of something heavy, clunky, and slow. You need to forget all of that because these carts fly! The engines on these racing carts are not taken from old lawn mowers and the frames are not made from angle iron used in old bed frames. These are snappy machines that can reach speeds of up to thirty-five or forty miles per hour — talk about wonderful flying machines!

This isn't a cheap hobby, but, the point is, this is something special that you will never forget.

If you are between the ages of eight and fifteen, you will need to take (and pass) a driving test. (Did I mention that these things fly?) You will be out on the track with other drivers who want that next corner just as bad as you do. Everyone wears a driving suit and a helmet. And everyone wants that checkered flag. And watch out for the quiet ones. They might be the real drivers; the ones who find that calm space on the track in the middle of the noise and the rumble thunder-shaking their bones.

Who doesn't crave the exotic smell of fuel and hot tires mixed with fear and adrenaline inside a converted warehouse? Who can tell what the building's former use may have been, it looks like just another grayish structure in an industrial park. But who knows, maybe the building was a button and bow distributor for the Northeast.

But not anymore.

Now the building is filled with revving engines, squealing tires, and smiles. Smiles that come from teetering on the brink, almost losing control, learning nuances, then pushing past the limit to a new best time. Or you might find that a cart will only stick to the pavement up to a certain speed, after that, the machine gets loose. The wheels drift. Then the rules totally change.

There is a delicate balance between control and speed and loosing control and crashing.

Then there is the gear: the driving suit, the head-sock, the helmet, and the neck collar. (Also, no open-toed shoes are allowed.) And then there is this matra that all instructors gush: Listen. Do.

A computer that keeps track of your fastest lap, average speed, number of laps, and the time for each lap in order, so you can see your progress. You get a printout of your run at the end of your race.

Maine Indoor Carting also doesn't want new drivers out there with more experienced ones until the former get their lap-times down. Nobody wants the young rookies racing with the Mad Maxes who come by on the way home from work to blow off a little steam.

These carts seriously stick to the tar. They have soft-compound tires that grip the pavement like they are on rails. They have snappy disc brakes, low centers of gravity, and enough power to pop you and your cart up to forty miles per hour in a space that's half the size of your average grocery store.

When you start driving into corners and drifting out into large sweepers, you feel the control getting thin and your brain tries to figure out the new rules, to stay right on the verge, but to not cross over. Your peripheral vision becomes one long blur. Ignore it. Nothing in that blur will help you go faster. And speed is the name of this game! The faster you go, the more you feel the cart. You wear it. The cart becomes part of you.

You stop looking just ahead because what's in front of you is behind you too fast to be of any help. In fact, you start looking so far ahead that when you first get out of the cart after a race, your first couple of steps feel awkward. And you feel like you're in a kind of time warp. In those eight minutes of racing you go somewhere else, into a world of speed and horsepower. Without the threat of state troopers and speeding tickets, you can immerse yourself into the world of racing, into the rawness of the bouncing cart, blasting into corners, exploding out, G-forces that make your neck tired as you try to keep your head from flopping around like a rag-doll's.

So the next time you think about go-carts, think fast and furious, not slow and laborious. ∎

22 The Roll Back

HAVE YOU EVER WONDERED WHAT ALL THOSE BLACK MARKS IN THE ROAD ARE? If you like mysteries to remain in the universe, you might not want to read this chapter.

Ever since I was a little kid I have wondered about these black marks. But then I started noticing marks that looked like the letter "J". I asked my dad. He told me: "Idiots back down a hill in their car, often it's not one they paid for, then they slam it into drive under full throttle."

My father, obviously, did not approve of the situation.

I now know that burning out and squealing tires come from applying too much power to the wheels than the tires have the friction to handle, causing the traction to fail and the tires to spin, leaving some of their rubber on the road.

On backcountry roads all over Maine you will see burn marks in the road. What to some are eyesores, to others are an art form of complicated patterns, almost like calligraphy. You need to look at these marks in the road like cave art. They are marks that record a moment in time when a mysterious driver

The Cost of Burning Tires

This activity can destroy a fifty-thousand-mile tire in one session. It puts a terrible strain on the transmission and the engine, which can lead to costly repairs. A tire can catch fire and burn the car to the ground. You might get a ticket, which could raise your insurance costs.

on a country road revved his engine. You also have to imagine the grin on that driver's face in the blue-green light of the dashboard, the smell of burning rubber, and the cloud hanging in the air as the sound of the engine fades into the night. ■

Burning Tributes

In March of 2007 a funeral director burned rubber with his hearse in front of the Camden Opera house in honor of Michael Libby. There were so many cars burning rubber on Route 1 that day, the smell started to fill the Opera House. When an eighteen-year-old Appleton fireman died in March of 2009, people gathered at the fire station for the memorial and some of his friends started burning rubber on the road in tribute.

Smokin'

The object of a burn-out competition is to be the first one to burn the tires off the rims. One competitor I spoke to had this to say about it: "It was really cool. After a while, the car was completely buried in smoke and we could hear the tires pop. I smelled so bad when I got home, my wife made me undress on the porch. She threw everything I was wearing in the trash."

Car Talk
The Nuts and Bolts of Burning Rubber

How on earth are those black marks in the road made?
You clamp off the rubber hydraulic line running back to the brakes with vice-grips so that when you stomp on the brake, only the front wheels are affected. Now that you have disabled your back brakes, you do a standard rollback, and when the car starts to move forward, you feather the brakes. Now you can burn those tires all you want!

But what about when the marks suddenly stop and then start going sideways?
Power braking. When you stomp on the brake, the front tires stop altogether — not just slowing the car — but the rear wheels keep spinning. The tires move to the side of least resistance, usually to the right, because of the way the road crowns in the middle. Now when a driver lets up a little on the brakes, away they go. With those squiggles, this time the driver just turns the front wheels this way and that while maintaining some resistance with the power braking. All this is done in low gear.

23 How to Build a Survival Shelter

EVERYONE IMAGINES THEY COULD FEND FOR THEMSELVES IN THE WILDS OF MAINE LIKE A ROBUST PIONEER OF OLD. But strip the average person of his or her electronic appliances, and chances are his or her survival skills will reduce in equal proportion to their lack of high-tech gizmos.

If you ever do find yourself alone in the Maine woods at night without a sleeping bag or tent, here's a simple survival shelter you can build to keep you safe and warm until you can get that iPhone signal again.

The idea with this shelter is that you can make it to stay warm and dry in sub-freezing conditions without any fire and using only your body's heat to keep you warm. And remember to build small to conserve body heat — small as in a mummy-style sleeping bag. Making a larger one will only waste precious heat.

The shelter starts with a simple frame. But the location needs careful consideration.

* Pick a high spot that is dry

* Don't build your shelter in a place that might turn into a small pond or is already damp

The Padding

Gather leaves for the bedding first. It's easier to make the leaf bed before the frame. Once you have a good pile of leaves, stomp on them. Then add more and repeat the stomping until you have a nice, dense mat of leaves, about 4 inches thick. Be selective with these leaves: pull out any sticks.

The Frame

The frame can be made with hoops of wood stuck in the ground:

* Make half-circle hoops a little taller than your body when you are lying flat on the ground.

* Weave straight saplings in and out along the length of the shelter.

Note: If saplings can't be found, your shelter can be made from larger, less flexible branches. In this case, find a spine for the structure. Prop it up with two crisscrossed supports. It needs to be fairly long so there will be enough room above your feet when you get all the way in your shelter. Then keep laying branches along its length until you get enough cover.

Stopping the Entrance

* Make a circle of saplings that fits the size of your shelter opening

* Weave small branches across it

- Pack lots of leaves on top of this circle

- Weave more saplings over the top of the leaves

There is nothing precise about the circle; it just needs to hold a bunch of leaves in a clump. Don't sweat this part too much. If you don't have the time or supplies to make this "door," just plug the hole as much as you can with leaves — anything you do in the way of more insulation and less airspace will keep you warmer than if you did nothing at all. ■

24 A Canoe and the Man Who Built One

EVERYONE AT SOME POINT IN HIS OR HER LIFE HAS A BIG DREAM. MINE WAS TO BUILD A BOAT.

I decided to start simple. So I looked at the coracle, the simplest boat imaginable. But they are terribly unstable. Although their circular design (about three feet in diameter) makes them light and easy to carry, it also makes them go in circles in the water, just like a water bug, spinning and going nowhere. It also requires a sculling motion for a primary paddling technique. They will go straight, but they will never go fast. They also require money for materials and more time than I think would be worth it. And, anyway, I kept thinking that for less than twenty bucks I could buy a kiddy pool at Renys, put a cheap circle of plywood in the bottom, and I would have a nice coracle!

Next I looked at building an authentic birch bark canoe. But I have seen people building these boats and just watching made me exhausted — it takes a great deal of skill, knowledge, and time to build an authentic birch bark canoe.

Next I thought: I have always wanted to build a kayak. Now

that's a boat worth the trouble. They can tackle big, exposed water and do it with speed and grace. But they require many hours and still require an infusion of cash for the materials.

Like most Mainers, I'm frugal, so I began to wonder about an easy and cheap slab boat made from a slab cut of pine. (The first cut that a lumber mill makes on a round log is to slab off the round part, to square the log up so flat boards can be cut from it.) The slab wood is generally considered inferior for most things, including firewood, because the outside of a tree consists of mostly sapwood. Sapwood has little resistance to bugs and rot and it's not the right shape to build with. So I scrapped that idea.

But then I found Michael Storer's plans on the Internet for a boat called the "Quick Canoe." The idea of a disposable canoe intrigued me. It's a boat that can be made quickly with simple tools and materials from the local hardware store or lumberyard. It was the perfect boat project.

Disposable Canoe Lore

The idea of a disposable canoe is not unique. The Native Americans built similar boats. If they had a mission — for war or for food gathering — they would send a team ahead to coordinate the boat building. Some would gather bark; some would gather and split the spruce root for sewing; some would build the form; some would split and bend the ribs; some would mix the wax and pitch to seal the seams. After the mission, the boat would either be discarded or hidden for a possible future use, or maybe ever destroyed if they thought that the boat might help the enemy.

The boat's economy comes from its construction method. Instead of "stitch and glue," a process of tying the hull together with copper wire through drilled holes, this boat uses "tape and glue." No need to drill holes. And there are no wires in the way when you glue the hull together. I used painter's masking tape and it only took me a half hour to tape the hull together.

I knew this boat wouldn't win any beauty pageants, but you can build it fast and inexpensively. I built it in my garage. At 15 ½ feet long, the canoe takes some space to build, so keep this in mind. I built the canoe over a month that added up to about two solid weekends of time. It's not a boat that will take heavy abuse. Most of the light wood boats, even the beautiful stripper canoes, don't do well with big white water.

But most of all, it works!

Building The Canoe

The Materials

❖ Three eight-foot sheets of ¼ inch plywood. I used ¼ inch plywood that had three plies that were the same thickness. This is important. Some ¼ inch plywood has a very thin veneer on the face and back. The middle ply is thicker. This makes it very weak, so pick plywood with similar ply thicknesses. I bought these for under $20 per sheet. Each sheet weighed about eighteen pounds.

❖ Epoxy glue. It costs more, but sticks better.

❖ Narrow strip of fiberglass to cover each joint for strength, waterproofing, and toughness.

❖ Marine paint (this took a quart of primer, a quart for the interior, and a quart for the outside). Using house paint could have saved some money, as the marine paint ran about $30 dollars a gallon. I took the marine route, however, because my plywood needed all the help I could give it to keep it waterproof.

Note: Marine plywood is far superior to ordinary plywood. It takes continuous submersion without the glue giving way — delaminating is the fancy term. But it costs as much as four times what wood from the hardware store costs.

The Process

1 Lay out the lines on the eight-foot long sheets of plywood

2 Cut them out with a jigsaw

3 The next step uses a simple but strong joint that is patched on the inside to join the eight-foot plywood together into sixteen-foot-long parts. When the epoxy dries (usually overnight), the two sides and the bottom measure almost sixteen feet long. My pieces wobbled and flexed so much, I worried they would snap in two when I picked them up to move them. But when I started taping the bottom to the sides with painter's masking tape, the boat gradually started taking shape. One roll of masking tape transformed the wobbly parts into a rigid hull that took on not only its own new structure, but it even had a sound of its own, not the dead and thunky sound of ¼ inch plywood, but a sharp, tight sound of a drumhead. It took less than a roll of masking tape and about thirty minutes for those plywood parts to become boat shaped, and for me to believe. Without epoxy or fiberglass or gunnels or thwarts or seats or knees, the dead pieces of plywood had become alive. The boat weighed about fifty pounds after the paint and seats. Lots of commercial canoes weigh more than seventy pounds. It took less than thirty total hours of work over about a month. ■

Great Places to Canoe

There comes a time in everyone's life when you need a canoe trip. Every time I'd go to Augusta, I'd see the Kennebec disappear below the bridge and wish I was paddling it.

❖ **The Allagash Wilderness Waterway** is recognized as one of the best canoeing areas in the country. Paddling north from Chamberlain Bridge there are more than one hundred miles of lakes and river. There are no dangerous rapids and navigation is not difficult, although some camping and canoeing experience is recommended. The longest trip through the waterway starts at Chamberlain Lake and ends at Allagash Village, a distance of about ninety-two miles and takes between seven and ten days.

❖ **The Kennebec River's** best section to paddle is from The Forks to Caratunk. The current is fast but with easy rips and Class 1 rapids for the first eight miles, then a mile of paddling on beautiful Wyman Lake to Caratunk. This fun canoe trip is about nine miles long and takes about three hours to complete. This is a great trip for beginners since the rapids are easy.

❖ **The Machias River** offers some of the finest white water. The river wends through the remote interior of eastern Maine and the route is characterized by glacial formations, white pine stands, and Arctic-like blueberry barrens.

❖ **The Saco River** offers 125 miles of clear, meandering water that supports a large number of recreational opportunities. The Saco River, named by Native Americans, means "flowing east." The 3.8 mile paddle between Swan's Falls and Canal Bridge is a popular route, and both areas serve as river access as well as a campground. There are many primitive camping spots along the river, such as white sandy beaches and sandbars, but respect the "No Trespassing" signs and carry out what you carry in.

❖ **The St. Croix River** (on the eastern Maine Canadian border). One of Maine's true gems, this river is guaranteed to provide the classic canoe trip. The river flows through beautiful woodlands and vast natural meadows. It features an abundance of easy whitewater and scenic, secluded campsites. The Saint Croix can be enjoyed by a wide range of canoeists, from beginner to expert. Noted as one of the few principal nesting areas for the bald eagle, it also has a significant moose population, and boasts superb smallmouth bass and salmon fishing.

❖ **The Saint John River** is considered the "granddaddy" of all Maine canoe trips and this canoe trip is the classic spring river trip in Maine's great North Woods. Rising in a series of remote ponds, the Saint John starts as a narrow stream, flows deep through dense coniferous forests of northwestern Maine, and eventually evolves into a river of majestic proportions. The river is quite suitable for novices; the white water increases gradually in difficulty from the riffles of the upper stretches to the heavier water of the renowned Big Rapids.

25 Making a Long Bow Like Robin Hood

OKAY, SO YOU HAVE NO AMBITION TO BE AN OUTLAW, BUT MAKING YOUR OWN REAL LONG BOW, WELL, THAT BEATS SHOVELING SNOW IN WINTER.

To make a proper bow, you need a good Maine tree. The tree should be at least four to five inches in diameter. Using a much larger tree is fine, but small trees are easier to come by, easier to cut down, and easier to split. If the tree is good and straight and the pith (the center circle of the tree) is centered, you might get two bows out of a four to five inch tree. We have several trees in Maine that work well. Sugar maple and hickory and ash all make excellent bows. But I talked to one primitive bow maker who likes hop hornbeam the best.

We are talking about making the long bow, specifically a self-bow (a bow made from one piece of wood); a primitive bow can be made with very few tools, but it's still a bow that is capable (when properly made) of dropping large game like deer.

Don't settle for lumberyard wood. Sawmills cannot see the grain of the wood and they cut through the tree's growth rings.

> The shaping of a bow is called "tillering." This should be done when the wood is dry. String the bow up often to test that the draw weight and length measures where you want it.

Wood from the lumberyard is also dried in a kiln. Your bow will be more lively if it dries at its own pace without the high temperatures that a kiln produces.

A good bow should measure from the ground to about your nose (in its unstrung form). So cut the tree a little longer than its finished length. The bark side of the tree will be the "back" of the bow, which strangely is the part of the bow that faces forward, toward your target. The "inside" of the bow, being on the opposite side from the back, is called the "belly."

Cutting the Bow

1 Split the tree in half lengthwise. You can do this with just an axe and a sledgehammer. If it doesn't split easily, make some wooden wedges out of good hardwood.

2 Now create your bow blank, which comes from the very outside of the tree. Try to split at least a two-inch-square chunk of wood from your tree for each blank. If the wood won't split evenly, you know early on and with very little time invested that it just wouldn't have made a good bow.

3 After you get your square blank, peel the bark off. Be careful not to cut or damage any of the wood under the bark. These fibers are under tremendous strain when the bow is drawn. The bow gets its energy by stretching the fibers of the back and compressing the fibers of the belly. The most important thing to remember is that the back of the bow (the part that was the outside of the tree) never gets shaped or cut. If you have a drawknife, it will make fast work of rough shaping. You could also just use a band saw.

Draw Weight

70-100 pounds	10-15# draw weight
100-130 pounds	15-25# draw weight
130-150 pounds	25-35# draw weight

If you want to hunt deer with any bow in the state of Maine, the bow needs to have at least 35# of pull and you need to shoot a broad head (one of those razor-headed arrows). If you weigh less than 150 pounds, you might have to buy a compound bow or shoot your deer with a rifle. The reasoning here is that the draw weight of a bow imparts a certain energy to the arrow. In theory, the higher the draw weight, the faster the arrow. But other factors influence arrow speed, like weight of the tips of the bow. A heavier tip will tend to move slower with the same amount of force, and so the string will propel the arrow with less speed.

Drying the Bow

A bow will not perform at its peak until it dries out, but if it dries too quickly, the wood can crack. If you shape your bow close to its final dimension, it will dry faster. If you wrap it up in paper, the bow can be brought into a dry environment, or put out in the sun from time to time without the wood cracking. Roll out enough paper for the length of your bow plus a foot on either side. Fold it in half. Tape the bottom and one side shut. Put your green bow in and roll up the open end. Now you have a safe place for your bow to dry at the proper rate. Now you can leave your bow in an unheated garage or shed and wait for it to finish drying. When your bow stops losing weight, it's ready. A bow dried in this way could be ready to shoot in a couple of months. You won't know your bow's true spirit and its power until it dries and you string it up. Take your bow to a local sporting goods store that specializes in archery equipment. They should be able to help you pick the proper string length.

Tillering Your Bow

After you string your bow, the true "tillering" begins. You can use a rasp or a spokeshave (needs to be very sharp) to bring your bow to its final shape. I have heard experienced makers speak with pride about using a drawknife for the whole shaping process, right down to the final tillering, but that is pretty advanced.

If the bow pulls too hard, thin the limbs. If one limb bends more easily than the other, thin just the limb that doesn't bend as easily. Go slow here.

When you get the bow properly tillered, it's time to sand and finish. I like a product called Tru-Oil. It's used on gunstocks, so it's tough. ■

Bow of the Brave

In 1660 a Wampanoag Indian armed with only his bow lost a battle to men with firearms. Although he died in the fight, his enemies thought enough of his long bow to preserve it. The bow eventually found its way into Harvard University's Peabody Museum. The bow measured sixty-seven inches long.

26 X Marks the Spot

IT IS SAID THAT THE SCOTTISH PIRATE WILLIAM KIDD SUPPOSEDLY BURIED TREASURE SOMEWHERE ALONG THE COAST OF MAINE. It may be true, but where are you going to look? And where can you plant a shovel without finding out you've trespassed onto someone's private beachfront?

There's a much simpler and easier way to find treasure in Maine. It's called geocaching (secret storage spots have long been called "caches," pronounced *cashes*) and it provides the same thrill as a pirate treasure hunt, but with a somewhat lowered expectation of wealth (you won't get rich geocaching). But the wonderful thing about geocaching is that not only does the treasure not get pillaged, but also there are items for exchange in some of the larger caches: these range from trading cards to foreign coins.

The idea for geocaching is you take an item from a cache and replace it with an item of similar value. Geocaching is really a modern, high-tech game of hide and seek. And there are more than six thousand active geocaches in the Pine Tree State, and

Maine's cachers create an average of about 2.5 new caches each day. There's even a Website: geocachingmaine.org/forum

To geocache you will need a GPS, a handheld device that tells you where you are on the planet in relation to everything else and defines every spot on the Earth with a longitude and latitude number. Then you need someone to hide a cache. The person hiding caches give the longitude (north, south) and latitude (east, west) coordinates, and a couple of clues about the cache. These clues could tell you the size of the item, how difficult the terrain is, and other pertinent information to help prepare you for your search.

Every cache has a logbook that you sign and date before returning the container to its hiding spot. The containers range in size from a micro-mini to something as big as an ammo box. The smaller caches contain just a log page to sign. Larger caches get more elaborate, with tokens to exchange, or trackable items. The trackable tokens are supposed to be taken and moved to another cache. The idea here is to have these items move from cache to cache so that people can watch where they travel. They could travel from an ammo box in Paris, Maine, to Paris, France. The owner of the trackable can see when and where it moves as people record the find and what they do with it.

Geocaching can work in two ways: It can be the primary focus: get some coordinates from geocaching.com that look interesting and go find them. Or you find yourself at a doctor's appointment and you have some time to kill so you use your Smartphone to log into Geocaching.com and find the coordinates of nearby caches. Or you're going on a long trip and you could find caches along the way.

More than nine thousand Maine geocaches have been placed since the first Maine cache was hidden in 2001. Some cachers place their caches deep in the woods. (These would not be an example of a cache you might do casually, but more of an all-day commitment.) The average time to find a cache is listed with the information, so you know how much time to expect to take, along with the things you will need, like a scuba tank, say. Some caches require extreme measures. If it says you need scuba gear, it's probably not the best one to attempt first. Start out simpler, with a cache that only requires walking boots. ∎

Space-Age Science

If the Soviets hadn't launched the *Sputnik 1* satellite in 1957, we might not be talking about geochaching in Maine. That first satellite has nothing to do with GPS (global positioning system), but the satellite broadcast a signal at a common frequency and physicists knew that the signals from the satellite traveled at the speed of light (186,000 miles per second). They also noted that the satellite's signal shortened as it approached and lengthened as it went away from the Earth. They ran various numbers that they had collected and a computer plotted the exact orbit of the satellite. This enabled the physicists to find the real-time position of the satellite in space. A couple months later, the navy heard about this satellite tracking and asked if the process could be reversed so an unknown point on the Earth could be found from a known satellite orbit. The navy did some math, launched some satellites of their own, and used this new technology to precisely locate submarines in the oceans. Thirty years later, the first GPSs were "opened up" to the public. Now these devices have an accuracy to within a couple feet. But without the launch of the *Sputnik 1* and the curiosity of young scientists in 1957, geocaching might not exist today.

27 Build a Stone Arch

GRAVITY IS THE GLUE THAT HOLDS THE UNIVERSE TOGETHER. It's also what holds together a simple stone arch on the beach.

We've all seen arches. They have been around since before the Roman Empire. The Romans perfected the arch, though, making it a decorative feature as well as a practical way to make an opening in a stone structure.

Build a stone arch on the beach and people will come to inspect it: they will come, they will see, they will leave in awe. Just as a stonemason must develop a vocabulary, a technique, to categorize the shapes of rocks, you, too, as a stone arch builder, will learn the drama of suspending odd-shaped rocks in the air with no mortar.

In order to build an arch, a form is needed, something that will hold the shape of the rocks. An arch needs two curves that hold each other up — you can make a form out of plywood that can be built in two pieces. While making a form out of plywood works, it also involves material and access to tools and the knowledge of their use. There is a simple method: use a beach

Singing Arches

You can build arches out of split firewood. Firewood is already in wedge-shape pieces. Or you could use larger rocks; snow blocks can make arches. If you can make an arch out of crazy beach rocks, you can make one out other materials. But try to build an arch that will withstand the tides. Remember, though, the beach arch, although more durable than a sand castle, is still a thing of the moment. Think of it like music playing or laughter.

ball. It's light, cheap, and doesn't take up much space. And it can be inflated and deflated to make many arches.

After the rocks are in place, test for loose fits. If you find unstable spots, now is the time to "shim" those loose spots with thin wedge rocks. They won't look pretty, but you will be amazed at what these little rocks can do to stabilize your arch. After your construction comes the moment of truth: Slowly let the air out of your beach ball and watch what happens. ■

One Rock at a Time

Things to keep in mind: Each rock needs solid placement and you must consider the next rock. Your structure only gets more unstable as you add rocks. Place each rock carefully. A rickety rock down near the bottom could ruin your arch. Start with a large, solid foundation. Avoid round rocks against round rocks. When shimming, use thin rocks, and tuck them in while listening and feeling. Sensitivity and arch building seem like they don't go together, but they do. Think about the line: Do the rocks on one side head straight toward the others, or do they have a curve? The straighter the better. Ideally each rock should form a wedge that points in the direction of the center of the beach ball.

28 Skipping Stones

SEEMS LIKE THERE WOULDN'T BE MUCH TO SAY ON THIS TOPIC. NEARLY EVERY-ONE HAS PICKED UP A STONE AND SKIPPED IT ACROSS THE WATER. Some go well, and some don't. End of chapter, right?

Not quite.

Like most simple things, even stone skipping has profound depths.

It may be hard to believe, but French physicist Lydéric Bocquet decided that he would write a doctoral thesis on the simple act of skipping stones. Here is what he found.

The most important thing is that you throw the stone so that it first hits the water at a twenty-degree angle. Any lower than that, and the stone loses too much energy to water-drag. Stones that hit the water at higher than a forty-five-degree angle go right through the surface and sink without ever bouncing back.

Home-Grown Skipping

Maine has its own annual stone-skipping contest that is held every July near the Boothbay Harbor Foot-bridge. The organizers ask for a donation of five dollars for adults and one dollar for children to compete (all money goes to the Boothbay Region Food Pantry). The competition started informally among friends in 2003 and they proclaimed their event the first International Rock Skipping Contest, and it has been going on ever since. Skips recorded in the twenties are commonplace. Currently Alex "Skip Masta" MacKay holds the contest record with twenty-eight skips. In recent years, the contest has attracted more than one hundred competitors. The rules require all contestants to have a rock-skipping nickname. You are also required to BYOR (bring you own rocks)!

The next important thing is spin. Bocquet's equations found that the ideal speed for skipping a rock is twenty-five miles per hour and that the stone should spin at fourteen rotations per second. (The spinning keeps the rock flat.) Bocquet and his team are building a machine that they hope will break the world record of thirty-eight skips. This record, authenticated by the *Guinness Book of World Records*, was set by a Texan engineer named Jerdone Coleman McGhee. He set his record on the Blanco River in Central Texas. It was verified by video at thirty-eight skips. His thirty-eight skips have even been recognized by NASSA (the North American Stone Skipping Association). Since the Texan skipper, the *Guinness Book of World Records* has now recognized Russell "Rock Bottom" Byars from Pennsylvania as making fifty-one skips. ■

The Art of Skipping

1 First thing to do is to choose a skipping stone. The stone should be as flat as possible and about the size of your palm. Plus it shouldn't weight more than a tennis ball. Also, triangular stones tend to skip best. Actually avoid circular stones, they seem to be less stable.

2 Grip the stone with your thumb and middle finger, firmly hooking your index finger along the edge of the stone — your thumb goes on the top of the stone.

3 Stand up straight and face the water at a slight angle. Try to maintain this position during your entire windup and release. The lower your hand is at the release, the better.

4 Now, it's time to release that stone. A skipping stone bounces off the water, so give it plenty of downward force. Spin it as hard as you can with a quick snap of your wrist. Keep in mind: strength is not the key, quickness is. So throw faster instead of harder. The stone should hit the water parallel to the surface.

29 Toss Some Apples

FALL IS THE PERFECT TIME IN MAINE TO FLING APPLES. FORGET BOBBING FOR THE FRUIT — WE'RE TALKING GOBLIN ANTICS AND IMPISH FUN HERE, BECAUSE THIS CHAPTER IS ALL ABOUT MAKING AN APPLE FLINGER. And it's so simple to make, even an ogre could do it.

Put a sharp point on the skinny end of a branch. But look for a branch that bends like a fishing pole. Then strip the leaves and skewer an apple on the sharpened tip. Voila! You are now a master apple flinger creator.

Okay, don't get too carried away just yet. There is more to learn about this messy art.

The age-old problem with apple flinging is the stick itself. Even after finding the perfect springy branch, the battle is not won. If the flex of your stick starts out great, it inevitably gets too rubbery to get that proper snap. Even if you start with a stouter stick, and it doesn't fatigue significantly, there is always the danger of it breaking because of an over-enthusiastic fling

Catapult Action
Never fling side arm — only overhead, like a catapult. This way you can control at least one variable fairly well: the direction of the apple.

or a too-heavy apple — or both. You now need to get a feel for the weight of the apple and the flex of the stick. But what an apple flinger lacks in accuracy, it more than makes up for in raw power.

Another variable that frustrates the art of apple flinging is that apples don't come in any standard weight. Also, the amount of force it takes for an apple to release can affect accuracy. Generally, the larger the apple, the greater the need to jam it farther down on the slick; the smaller the apple, less the need to shove. If the apple is on too tight, it will release too late — splat on the ground in front of you — or not at all. An apple that is too loose flies off behind you. But once you get the hang of it, you can throw for power, about head high and parallel with the ground, or distance, with a trajectory of about forty-five degrees. The reward for your patience and practice is the sound of that apple whistling off the stick and disappearing from sight and the silent seconds waiting for the quiet thud or thunk. But be careful where you throw: you are responsible for that apple missile.

There really is some truth to that old folklore about an apple a day keeps the doctor away — especially if that apple is tossed. ∎

Fishing for the Best Flinger

A fishing pole with a broken-off tip is the best tool for flinging apples. An old fishing pole (the upper half) with the top eyelet broken off eliminates the fatigue issue and the flinger changing stiffness (or breaking) along the way. Also the tip will remain consistently sharp instead of becoming blunt or splintered with use.

30 Rat Hunting

OKAY, SO YOU'VE SEEN THAT ANIMATED MOVIE *RATATOUILLE* AND NOW YOU THINK EVERY RAT IS AS ADORABLE AS REMY.

But rats can also be a nuisance — remember the bubonic plague of the fourteenth century.

It's true, rats have gotten a bad rap. But, hey, *Rattus* has brought on a lot of its own negative publicity. It also doesn't help that rats dig their burrows anywhere. They are fond of digging even when they have a well-established system of dens and underground tunnels. And if you keep chickens, a growing backyard hobby in Maine, then sooner or later you will have to deal with a pack of rats.

So, what are you options? You could use rat poison, but the anticoagulant causes a slow, painful death. Plus rats never die in

Ratted Out

When you're dealing with *Rattus norvegicus,* also known as the brown rat or sewer rat or wharf rat, you need to know that they breed like crazy. In their dark burrows, things are getting tough for the rats. They are running out of space, maybe having trouble getting enough food. What you have there is a stressed-out rat colony. Not good. So maybe you catch a couple in traps. But then the others become trap-smart. Rats are neophobic (afraid of anything new) by nature . . . but dead rats in traps. Rats aren't stupid! If you are going to trap, the only way to do this is to set lots of traps, think twenty or more, and make sure to bait them every night for a couple weeks. But don't set them. Then one night: *kablam, kablam, kablam.* It's the only way.

the open; they scamper back to a burrow or die in some hard-to-get place. And a full-grown rat can weigh as much as a pound and a half. That's a lot of rat to rot away! Then there's other wildlife to consider, like owls and hawks and even feline pets, who might want to make a meal of the poisoned rat. Or you can ignore the critters.

But you could try hunting them. There's no season. No bag limit. No licensing or fees. And nobody seems to object to the killing of rats. Even my vegan friends don't mind my rat hunting. ■

King Rat

My way of hunting rats is with a rifle. My wife wasn't keen on a gun in the house. But she hated the rodents more. First I looked at air rifles. My head swam with the various specifications and costs. They don't need a background check; cost only a few cents a shot; and are fairly quiet. But in the end, I decided on a classic .22 semiautomatic rifle because of its wide variety of ammunition, which are pennies a shot. The automatic can be loud or quiet, depending on ammunition. (So keep your neighbors in mind.) The 22 high-velocity hollow point rounds automatic really pack a wallop. I bought a bargain-model scope for under fifty dollars, but then spent almost that again for the scope mounts. I have thought about a game camera with a motion sensor and alarm with a remote link to my computer screen. But is it really hunting with all that technology? Some of the thrill of rat hunting comes from being still for long periods of time, watching as a rat steals the food scraps set out for it, the rat's metallic eyes reflecting in the dark . . . before you squeeze the trigger. The hollow-point bullet crosses the forty-five feet. The journey takes thirty-six thousandths of a second. The rat slumps. You walk over. A perfect kill.

31 The Moxie Rocket

IT LOOKS LIKE A NORMAL TWO-LITER BOTTLE INVERTED AND JAMMED ONTO A $1/2$ INCH PVC PIPE AND FILLED TWO THIRDS OF THE WAY WITH WATER. You might hear the bottle click under the tremendous pressure, and there may be a faint trickle of water running down the pipe, but, asides from that, the situation looks almost innocent. It's not. This is a rocket! And the seventy-five pounds of air pressure inside the bottle wants to get out. Bad. And when you pull the trigger, the pressure blows the water out of the nozzle and the rocket takes off, like a dragster, leaving a plume of water as it climbs above the trees. Then it floats for an instant, before floating back to earth.

This rocket starts with emptying a fresh two liter plastic bottle of Moxie, its fizz factor intact. A bottle that has been dented, folded, left in the sun, or opened, will make a less than satisfactory rocket.

And always remember to use caution! You're going to put lots of potential energy into this rocket. The bottle manufacturers say that an undamaged bottle should be fine up to a hundred pounds of pressure. I have seen many examples of bottles holding more pressure, but over a hundred pounds the risk of failure (nice way of saying explosion) go up.

A Moxie bottle can be used many times. Unless the rocket gets stuck in a tree or lands in the road and gets run over by a cement truck, it should be good for many launchings. Now you need to head to the hardware store for supplies (see "Moxie Rocket Materials").

Once you have the other materials, start by inserting the PVC pipe all the way to the bottom of the bottle, then pull it back out an inch or two. Use a pen to mark all the way around the pipe at the top of the neck. Take the pipe out, hold the marked ring over a candle flame, and rotate it slowly and evenly over the flame. It will probably turn black, that's okay. Keep rotating until the pipe softens and can bend easily. Heat it a bit more, then, while the pipe is still soft, try to push both ends together, like you are trying to shorten the pipe. Watch the section that the candle has blackened, it should bulge slightly. Keep the pipe straight until it cools. Slide the pipe back in the bottle. It should stop at the "swollen knuckle" you just made. And it should fit tightly — this will seal the air in the bottle

Next, drill a hole in the center of the end-cap so it's just large enough for the inner-tube valve stem. With scissors, cut a circle around the valve stem a little smaller than the inside of the end-cap. Put some silicone around the base of the stem. Push it into the hole, making sure it seals, squishing out the silicone. Now carefully prime the end farthest from the bulge with PVC primer according to the directions. Do the same with the inside of the end-cap that has the valve stem silicone inside of it. Apply PVC cement to both the primed parts. Put the cap on the end of the pipe. Jam the bottle onto the bulge. Put a rubber band on the pipe a couple inches below the bulge. Slide the twist ties under the rubber band with the head of the zip-ties over the flange on the neck of the bottle. Pull all the ties down so that each is firmly against the flange. Open the hose clamp enough to slide over the end-cap and up over the zip-ties. Tighten the hose clamp. Take the bottle off. Slide the 2-inch coupler down over the zip-ties. Put the bottle back on. Slide the flange under the zip-ties. Try out the trigger. Make sure it holds the bottle flange snug to the bulge. Adjust the fit of the bottle against the bulge. It needs to be tight to keep the air in. Once adjusted, tighten the hose clamp and you are ready to hook up the pump to see if you have a good seal and a properly adjusted trigger. ■

Moxie Rocket Materials

- ✔ 2-foot section of ½ inch PVC pipe
- ✔ End cap for ½ inch pipe
- ✔ PVC primer and cement (you don't need much of this as you only need to glue on the end cap, so try to borrow this)
- ✔ 8-inch electrical zip-ties
- ✔ Hose clamp large enough to go around the PVC pipe
- ✔ 2-inch PVC coupler
- ✔ Old bicycle inner tube — you only need the stem so the condition of the rest of the tube doesn't matter
- ✔ A small amount of silicone glue
- ✔ Bicycle pump, the kind with an air pressure gauge built in

32 Maine Roller Derby

A roller derby game is called a "bout." Maine Roller Derby bouts are family friendly and include live entertainment, witty announcers, raffle prizes, merchandise, and lots of very vocal fans. Bouts have two, thirty-minute periods with half-time entertainment.

WHEN I WAS A KID, PEOPLE SKATED DER-BIES ON BANKED TRACKS. And those tracks were expensive — not every community could afford them, so derbies were limited to a few who skated on television. And although it was athletic, it was not really a sport. It was like professional wrestling today — it was more of a theatrical show than an athletic event.

Things have definitely changed in the world of roller skating. Roller Derby is one of the few full-contact sports exclusively for women. These girls are not professional skaters, but they skate for the love of the sport, not for money. These ladies are boat captain, bankers, schoolteachers, and artists. Lots of them are moms. This flat-track style of derby skating has taken the nation by storm. And Maine has its own league, Maine Roller Derby, that is a member of the WFTDA (Women's Flat Track Derby Association).

A derby can be skated in a warehouse, in a convention center, even on a high school basketball court. Since there is no more need for special facilities, women everywhere can join a local league, get a pair of skates, and become skating warriors. Theses bouts are not "fixed." The hits are real. Concussions, knee and ankle injuries are part of the territory. But there is something beautiful mixed in with all the tattoos and piercings, strange outfits, and heavy mascara: there is a feeling of camaraderie out there. When the play is on, the girls skate with a reckless passion. But after the bout, you see players from opposing sides talking and laughing together.

There is a carnival feeling that comes alive when you attend a bout at the Portland Expo. And the players come in all shapes and sizes: some are small, but very fast on their skates. Some of the players on the track look like they are over six feet tall and at least two hundred pounds.

But then that's what puts Roller Derby in a class of its own. It's another world, and it's always worth the price of admission. ■

Maine has three Roller Derby Teams: The Port Authorities, the Calamity Janes, and the R.I.P. Tides.

It's All in a Name

Here are few of the most flavorful and strange monikers of the skating warriors:

Cherry Clobber	Mother Bones
Princess Layher Out	View Grinder
Wrex Zilla	Dubliner Broozes
Punchy O'Guts	Thigh Tanic
Crystal Whip	Curve Appeal
Li'l Punisher	

Pick a Position

A Roller Derby's full lineup for a bout consists of one pivot, three blockers, and one jammer. Each team may field up to five players for each bout.

Pivot: The pivot blocker wears a helmet cover with a stripe and she generally starts at the first starting line and serves as the leader of her teammates playing in a bout. Most teams play the pivot position at the front of the pack, so this position is the last line of defense to stop an opposing jammer from escaping the pack.

Blocker: The three blockers don't wear helmet covers. All blockers may play offense and defense at any given time and frequently switch between offensive and defensive tasks.

Jammer: The jammer wears a helmet cover with a star on it. She lines up at the second starting line and begins play at the second start whistle. The jammer's goal is to pass opposing blockers and emerge from the pack as quickly as possible. If she is the first of the two jammers to escape the pack without committing any penalties, she gains the strategic advantage of being able to stop the bout at any time by placing her hands on her hips. Once a jammer laps the pack, she begins scoring one point for every opposing blocker she passes legally. She can continue to lap the pack for additional scoring passes for the duration of the bout.

33 Pond Hockey

LIVING IN MAINE, PLAYING HOCKEY ON A POND IS JUST PART OF GROWING UP HERE.

You find some polished surface of ice and someone brings a flask of cocoa, and the puck starts to slide.

But pond hockey differs from rink hockey in a number of ways. Ponds and lakes freeze for free. There is no Zamboni guy honking his horn after fifty-nine minutes of ice time! You only have to stop play if the ice melts or gets too torn up from skates. Plus with pond hockey, there are no coaches and the rules can be made up as you go.

Pond hockey is a simpler game and it depends on quickness and puck handling skills, not brute force and hard shots. Accuracy is rewarded, as you can see by looking at how the goal is constructed. If you miss the hole, the puck bounces away from the goal and back into play. There is magic out there, to be certain, but make sure that the ice you want to play on is thick enough. Use an axe or hatchet to chop a hole to find out how thick the ice is. Ice should be at least four inches thick every *where you are skating* to be safe.

Rink Ice

Ice at indoor rinks is only a couple inches thick. Here is how they make it: First they make a light coat of ice. When this hardens, they apply a special white paint. Logos, artwork, and other lines are applied on top of the white and the whole thing is sealed up under a couple inches of plain ice to cover and protect the painted layer. The Zamboni has a big sharp blade that scrapes off the old surface at the same time that it mops new water on to renew the surface. A typical surfacing takes almost two hundred gallons of water. The Zamboni has four-wheel drive. All the tires have metal studs for traction.

Here is the official U.S. Pond Hockey Championships tour- nament rules:

✤ All players must wear helmets and hockey skates. Protective equipment is optional but highly recommended.

✤ No goalie equipment or goalie sticks permitted.

✤ Six referees will have the discretion to award a "penalty shot" to the opposing team when a minor penalty is flagrant and/or a team is consistently playing in a reckless manner.

✤ A penalty shot will be taken from the center of the ice and must be attempted within thirty seconds of the penalty being called. Anyone on the opposing team can take the shot. The team that is awarded the penalty shot will also be given possession of the puck following the penalty shot attempt (regardless of the outcome of the shot).

✤ Any major penalty, which includes any action that could possibly injure another player, will result in that player being ejected from the tournament. The team that received the ejec- tion will play the remainder of the tournament short-handed (3 vs. 4). Off-ice pond officials will determine major penalties.

✤ Abuse of officials will be considered a major penalty. This includes yelling, swearing, or arguing about calls.

✤ No checking is allowed. Such action will result in a minor penalty unless deemed serious enough to be a major penalty.

✤ No slap-shots allowed. Such action will result in a minor penalty.

✤ Players cannot fall or lay on the ice in an effort to protect the goal area. Such action will result in a minor penalty.

✤ Goaltending is not allowed. A player may not patrol or "camp out" or remain stationary in the crease — the crease area is defined as an imaginary box extending out four feet from the outside corners of the goal — area and act as a goaltender. A defender may deflect the puck in the crease area, but the defender must do so while continuing to move through the crease area.

✤ Contacting the puck with a stick above the waist will result in a loss of possession.

Hockey Skates

Skates need sharpening from time to time. Outside ice, especially if it's near a road where dust and salt might blow across it, can ruin edges fast. Skates get dull in the rink as well, it just takes longer. If you look very closely, the blades actually have a hollow — skate sharpeners define this in terms of a radius, which can range from 3/8 inch to 1 ½ inches; most kids skate with ½ inch radius. You need to sharpen your skates if they slip out when you corner. You can test them by dragging your fingernail lightly *across* the blade. If it scrapes a bit of your nail dust on both sides, they are sharp. If the blade slides *across* your nail with no resistance, they need sharpening. They also need sharpening if you see or feel nicks (by running your nail *along* the edge). You can check to make sure your skates are properly sharpened by holding the skate blade up, straight up and down (what a carpenter calls "plumb") and laying something straight on the blade. You could use a coin in a pinch or the back side of a credit card, but a small straight edge is preferable as it will make any error easier to see. The blade and the straight edge should be at right angles (ninety degrees to each other). If the straight edge is at an angle, your skating will suffer. Take them back and point this out to the person who sharpened them. Sometimes the machine is set for a different thickness of skate blade and will give your skates crooked edges. There are a number of reasons that the edges might be at an angle; the operator might have been in a hurry, or may have centered his sharpening stone on your blade, but your edges generally don't go dull evenly (the inside edge usually dulls faster because skaters generally use this edge more and harder than the outside). What matters is that the edges are even. No sense trying to relearn to skate with your skates improperly sharpened. You need a real machine (eight hundred dollars and up) to properly sharpen skates, so don't try to sharpen them at home on your dad's grinder. It won't work.

❖ Saucer passes (i.e., pucks that are lifted low, below the knee) are acceptable.

❖ If a puck goes out of bounds, the last team to touch it loses possession. During restart, the defender must give his opponent two stick lengths of space.

❖ There are no off-sides or icing calls.

❖ Teams must give their opponents half ice after a goal is scored or an infraction takes place.

❖ Games will be composed of two, fifteen-minute halves with a two-minute halftime.

❖ All games are running-time and substitutions can be made during play ("on-the-fly") or while a puck is being retrieved. There is no stoppage of play after a goal is scored, or after a penalty is awarded. It is up to each team to ensure that there are only four players on the ice.

❖ Generally there is no goalie in pond hockey. As you can see from the rules, players must be in motion when they are in front of their own goal.

❖ This simple goal takes the place of the goalie.

❖ Less equipment is needed if you follow the rules of pond hockey, because checking (smashing your body into another player) is not allowed.

❖ Slap-shots are not allowed.

❖ Pucks cannot be lifted higher than the knee. ■

34: How to Keep a Knife Sharp

MY UNCLE, WHO IS A WOODCARVER, USED TO TELL ME: "A SHARP KNIFE IS SAFER THAN A DULL ONE."

The thought behind this is that a sharp knife takes less force to do its job. Also, a sharp knife has less tendency to slip. So, on those two counts, the sharp knife is the safer knife.

The most important thing to keep in mind when using a knife (or any sharp tool) is where it will go if it slips. If you always keep this in mind, you will probably never cut yourself. I have heard people say "you should never cut toward yourself," but a controlled cut toward yourself should never present a danger if you keep the thought "where will this blade go if the wood disappears?" A controlled movement is one where the blade moves whether the wood is there or not. So when you use a knife, try to use controlled motions: try to move the knife at the same speed whether in the wood or in the air.

In my career as a woodworker, I have come across many methods of sharpening. People can be passionate about their

> **Sandpaper Grit**
>
> The number on the paper indicates how many particles occupy one square inch of sandpaper. A good place to start is 400 grit, then 600, then 1,200. Start with 400 to quickly shape the edge of a knife and get rid of all the nicks. While doing the initial work with the 400, take a look down the edge. If you can see glints of shiny spots, you need to keep working it. Once the shiny spots are gone, move on to the 600. After a couple of minutes on the 600, do the same thing with the 1,200, doing your best to keep the angle consistent. Remember, this takes practice.

sharpening technique. But let's look at what a sharp edge really is — in theory, it is just two planes that intersect at nothing. In the real world, however, these two planes come together to almost nothing by scratching the hardened steel of the blade's edge. If you were to look at the edge of a knife under a microscope, even a surgically sharp blade will look like a pile of cornflakes when there should be a clean intersection of two planes.

Now you could spend lots of money on fancy sharpening stones. Over the years I have bought oilstones, Japanese water stones, diamond stones, buffing wheels, and polishing compounds. They all work, but now I mostly use sandpaper. The wet/dry kind that they sell in the marine or automotive stores works best. This method will get a blade as sharp as you could possibly want.

You also need a flat surface (a small, thick piece of glass works well) and a piece of leather (a belt works fine) when sharpening a blade.

To start sharpening, set your knife blade down on one of its flat sides. Notice the gap under the edge. It's very small. Rock the knife until that gap goes away. Remember what this angle looks like, what it feels like to your hand and body. Good sharpening is about keeping this angle consistent as you are scratching the steel down to a very fine edge.

Now wet the sandpaper and put it down on the piece of glass. The water should make it stick to the glass and keep it from slipping after the paper soaks up the water. The paper may slide around at first but give it time to absorb the water. Water also allows the metal particles to float in the water as you cut them off. This keeps the sandpaper from clogging. If it clogs with metal particles, it will stop cutting.

You also need to choose a grit of sandpaper that matches your needs. If the edge of your knife is very dull, you will need to take off a good amount of metal to get the blade sharp. If your knife has nicks, start with a coarse grit — maybe 120 or 220, to get rid of the damage. If it is just dull, try starting at 400 grit.

The key to a good job is keeping a consistent angle as you move from one grit to the next. The best way to move the blade is toward the edge, like you are trying to cut the sandpaper. This helps to cut off the "wire edge," which is a very thin, ragged piece of metal that forms as you define your sharp edge. The goal is for the sandpaper to cut this wire edge off, not just fold it back and forth. You stand a better chance of cutting it off if you push the cutting edge over the sandpaper instead of dragging it back.

When you have gone through to 1,200 grit, you will have a very sharp knife. But if you run your fingernail (lightly!) down the edge, you will feel resistance. The next step is to polish the edge. You can make the edge sharper and last longer if you "strop" it.

Use your leather for this, but now drag the blade backward (if you push it forward as you did with the sandpaper, you will cut through and need a new belt). Work one side of the knife, then the other, back and forth, trying to keep the same angle as you did with the sandpaper. Do this several times, then test by dragging your fingernail down the edge again. It should slide much easier now.

When the knife gets a little dull, you can take a couple of passes on the strop and that should bring the sharpness back. Eventually you will need to take it back to the sandpaper, to make the edge crisp again as the belt tends to round it over after a while.

One of the best ways to test for sharpness is to try the knife on a piece of wood.

Do not run your thumb down the edge to test it. This test will only help to discover if you have blood in your thumb. Another test is to run your thumb across the blade. If you can feel the edge "catching" in the very small groves of your fingerprint, you can assume that the edge is very thin. If it is dull, the edge will be thicker and rounded, and you will not be able to feel the fingerprint grooves. ■

35 The Woodcock

I'VE WRITTEN A LOT IN THIS BOOK ABOUT GOING SOMEPLACE, DOING SOMETHING, MAKING SOMETHING, FINDING SOME-THING. These are all good things. But some of the best experiences in Maine are the ones that can happen by accident. You just happen to be around when a coyote lopes across that last sheet of crusty snow left in the corner of a field. You watch as he frantically digs, then pops his snow-crowned head out to listen, then pounces again, digging up more snow. Probably because he senses a meal under that snow; a mouse perhaps. It's not a thing that someone can tell you how to be prepared for. It just happens.

One day something odd caught my eye as I was out walk-ing a trail by my house. Spring had come, but snow still cov-ered everything in the woods. I spotted something brown and feathered with a long beak that looked like it might catch in the ground. And its body moved about in a strange dance. I was pretty sure that I had discovered some new and unique species, maybe even a last of its kind!

My wife knows about birds so when I got home I told her about the odd bird, about the beak, the strange dance.

"There's only one thing with a beak like that," said my wife matter-of-factly. "It's a woodcock."

And just like that, the magic drifted away like wood smoke in a breeze. For a while my wife's flawless observation got me down.

My wife noted my mood. "That dance," she said, "can you do it?"

I did, right there in the kitchen, although to do it real justice, I felt like I needed some bellbottom pants and a silky shirt.

"That's the woodcock's mating dance," she said. "There must have been another woodcock nearby."

Hope and magic flew back into the world. Here was a solitary woodcock just going about his natural spring ritual of looking for a mate with his crazy dance. And I was able to witness it just a short walk from my house.

Maine is a place where magic like this happens every day. ■